THE CREATIVE ROLE OF INTERPERSONAL GROUPS IN THE CHURCH TODAY

The Creative Role of

Interpersonal Groups
in the Church Today

Edited by John L. Casteel

ASSOCIATION PRESS, NEW YORK

For . . .

> JANE ELIZABETH
> LEIGH MARGARET
> CLARK CHRISTOPHER

> > . . . Three in
> > grandfather's
> > group

Preface

Ten years ago I had the privilege of editing and contributing to a book about personal groups. The purpose of that symposium was to make available some account of the various kinds of small groups then springing up in the churches.

The response to the book surprised those who were responsible for it. Many more personal groups were active in the churches and in movements more or less loosely connected with the churches than had been supposed. Moreover, a strong interest in the creation of such groups, hardly anticipated, was indicated by the wide reading the book has received.

In retrospect, this interest in personal groups would appear to be one of the manifestations of the general concern then in the air for the renewal of the churches. It shared the somewhat naïve expectations of a renewal movement that were to be found in the springing up of retreat centers, disciplined orders, and new forms of church life and ministry.

After a decade, some of the naïveté of the renewal trend has waned. Ventures begun in high hope with boldly proclaimed goals and exacting disciplines have gone out of business. Many of the vigorous groups of a few years ago have come upon arid days or ceased to exist, including some of those described in the book of ten years ago. Once again it becomes clear that the kingdom does not come by observation or even amateur zeal.

Nevertheless, the forces pushing the churches to some kind of renewal of their life and mission continue unabated. There are indications that the movement for such renewal has taken on larger dimensions, grown more worldly-wise about the obstacles to be overcome and the resource available for the

task, and, in particular, become more aware of the indispensable need of the development of mature persons as agents of
the renewal sought.

These developments raise in a fresh way the question of the
rationale for interpersonal groups, and of their potential contribution to the churches in this time of their crucial engagement with the world. If a second symposium on interpersonal
groups is to be offered, the book must give evidence of a con-
sciousness of this new situation and must point to the significant gains that have been made in the past decade in our
understanding of what such groups can be, how they function,
and the variety of circumstances in which they can be effective.
Three requirements would seem to call for recognition:

1. The book must represent the more important new varieties of
   interpersonal groups at work today, both inside and outside
   the churches.
2. It must be knowledgeable as to the basic insights and principles
   governing group functions that have been made available
   through research, experimentation, and experience.
3. It must be modest in its goals, recognizing how much, or little,
   can be done by one book in helping readers to become effective
   group leaders and members.

The present book tries to respond to these demands in two
ways: (1) It takes as a goal that of *illustration*—of pointing to
new developments in group theory and experience, so that
readers can know something of what is going on in the field
and may be motivated to undertake further study and experiment for themselves. (2) It undertakes, therefore, to report a
variety of group experiences, and to provide some exposition
of underlying principles for these experiences. Readers can at
least begin to see that the activities of interpersonal groups
have to do with more than simply a coffee pot, goodwill, and a
piety-of-the-Holy-Spirit. Some readers may be discouraged by
what is said and reported here. If so, the injunction that no
man should begin to build a tower without first reckoning the
cost may again be not amiss.

Yet it may be said that we have not yet begun to discover the full potentialities of interpersonal groups in contemporary living, and there is room for all who will take the risks and have the heart to go ahead, even where the way is not very clearly marked.

—JOHN L. CASTEEL

Contents

1. The Rise of Interpersonal Groups

JOHN L. CASTEEL

The author's professional career has been spent mainly in
university and seminary teaching, in the fields of speech,
homiletics, and practical theology. He has been active in a
number of religious movements and associations in which
group processes were widely used. Out of this background he
edited an earlier anthology, *Spiritual Renewal Through Personal Groups*. At present, he is a secretary on the staff of the
Council for Lay Life and Work of the United Church of
Christ, with responsibility for helping lay people think
through their own theological understandings. This chapter
sketches some of the trends in the rise of interpersonal groups
as a form of social behavior today and some of the causes contributing to this rise.

The rise and spread of interpersonal groups in our society has
been so rapid and so pervasive that many are unaware of its
extent or significance. Yet an increasing number of observers
would say, with Paul Hare, "Everywhere I turn the small group
is being rediscovered." [1] Almost every one belongs to one or
more relationships of the kind that Charles Cooley, more than
fifty years ago, gave the name "Primary Groups": relationships
characterized by "intimate face-to-face association and co-opera-
tion," exemplified by the family, the circle of school friends,
the gang, or the neighborhood.[2]

The groups now penetrating our social order go beyond
these more or less given relationships. They tend to arise out
of settings or relationships more or less voluntary in character.
They come into being by the free choice of their members, for
the purpose of expressing a common value or advancing a com-

mon goal or interest. Even those groups that are not entirely voluntary, such as the associations a man enters when he joins a company management or research team, are still characterized by interpersonal dimensions not entirely described by Cooley's analysis.

What are the forces and tendencies that have led to this rise of interpersonal groups today? A complete answer to this question cannot be given on the basis of such data as is now available. Those who have been most deeply involved in this group movement have been more preoccupied with studying and experimenting with its characteristics than with reflection upon its underlying causes. Out of the indications available, however, some conjectures can be raised. Five tendencies will be summarized here as either describing or, in some degree, accounting for the rise of the interpersonal group movement.

Basic Units

1. *Interpersonal groups are becoming the basic units for carrying on the functions of our society.* Primary groups are displacing the individual as the functional unit in a wide variety of situations and operations. In corporation structures, the solitary executive gives way to the management team.[3] Advertisements aimed at recruiting scientists, technicians, and engineers emphasize the "team concept" in the corporation's style of operation. One firm of stockbrokers dismantled its private offices for executives, and seated them around a kind of seminar table, where they would be instantly and continuously available for the kind of group decision making their functions required. "The Group" designates not only Vassar graduates but advertising studios, insurance underwriters, and medical practitioners. A new process for increasing potential creativity in solving theoretical and technical problems, called "Synectics," depends upon the small group as its basic working unit.[4]

In scientific research the group has become the operating unit. Although the great scientist still emerges, at rare intervals, as the unique genius, scientific experiment is more and more the venture of a collaborating team. The genius of the great atomic physicist, Niels Bohr, lay not only in his capacity to grasp as by insight the implications of a new hypothesis but also in his capacity to work exuberantly with the team of colleagues and students he gathered about him in his Institute in Copenhagen.[5] The export of theoretical physics to less developed countries is difficult, if not impossible, because theoretical research calls for a group of scientists who meet almost daily to talk over the problems and possibilities that engage them—and such groups do not exist, as yet, in many of these countries.

Group collaboration has not come into prominence as yet in the humanistic fields. Although the graduate student in the physical and—increasingly—the social sciences carries on his research as part of a project mounted by a team of faculty and students, the graduate student in the humanities tends to pursue his solitary studies in his library carrel, from which he issues occasionally to defend a paper in seminar. This difference in process may account in part for some of the difference in the vitality and significance of the graduate study issuing from these two fields. In theology the first hints are appearing that theological enterprise may again return from the dominance of the individual theologian to the activity of theological groups. Professor Edward LeRoy Long suggests that advance in the field of ethics may come through such a process. "Complementarity and mutual correction," carried on through continuing interchange among exponents of various ethical systems, will supplant fixed ethical codes.[6]

We have noted the rise of the group as the unit in which advances in theory and practice are taking place. A counterpart resort to small groups can be observed among the helping professions. Alcoholics Anonymous has been a forerunner among group movements that aim at helping individuals meet and overcome their problems—Divorcees Anonymous, Parents Without Partners, Synanon (for drug addicts), and TOPS ("Take Off Pounds Safely" for the obese), being illustrative.

Group therapy is becoming more and more widely practiced in the treatment of emotional problems.[7]

The development of groups and group process in educational methods, especially for adults, deserves a whole study for itself. In one large university Continuing Education Program for Adults, the most effective pattern for many courses, especially in the humanities, was found to be the informal setting of a home parlor; and the most effective teaching process that in which the professor met with the group on alternate weeks, to clear up questions, give needed new information, and set the discussion for the following meeting under leadership of members of the class.

And, to go beyond our own society, it may be noted that the group approach has been taken over as the basis of the "Rinsho Kosei Kai," a Buddhist lay society in Japan. "Hoza"—circle discussion groups—propagate and apply Buddhist teaching to life situations encountered by the lay members.

Without accumulating more evidence, it seems safe to say that the instances given point unmistakably to the way in which interpersonal groups are becoming the familiar and basic structures through which more and more aspects of our living enterprise are carried on in widening sectors of society.

Expanding Research

2. *Interpersonal groups have called forth an expanding body of research into group theory and practice.* In the rise of any important movement, the study of its characteristics and the application of theory to practice can be seen both as a consequence of the movement's rise and as the means through which this rise is accelerated. This certainly is true of the rise and expansion of the group movement. Research in the field, as Hare has shown, takes on the dimension of an "information explosion." In psychology, sociology, and related behavioral fields, group functions have become a central focus for investigation.[8]

Interest in group theory and practice goes back to the early

years of this century. In "The Inquiry," group thinking was
seen as essential to a democratic society. The writings of John
Dewey, especially his *How We Think*,[9] provided foundations
for this movement, as did the work of Mary Follett.[10] Harrison
S. Elliott's *The Process of Group Thinking* [11] worked out the
philosophy of this movement into practical procedures.

The chief characteristic of this approach to group behavior
was its emphasis upon the *thinking* function of the group
process. Although emotion was recognized as an accompaniment of group behavior, it was regarded more as an infrequent
interruption into the process than as a constant, central, and
inescapable aspect of it. Problem-solving was the goal of the
group process and made it indispensable to the democratic way
of life.

Group procedure began to be used in religious circles in the
years after the First World War. Bible study through group
discussion was popular among student movements and religious organizations. At a deeper level, the implications of the
interpersonal for religion were foreshadowed in John Mac-
Murray's *The Structure of Religious Experience*.[12] "The religious attitude," he wrote, "is that attitude of mind for which
our relations to other people are central. . . . For such an
attitude the main business of life consists in understanding,
appreciating, and creating the full reality of personal relationship." This point of view was to be developed, nearly twenty
years later, as the thesis of MacMurray's Gifford Lectures for
1954, *Persons in Relation*.[13]

Current approaches to group behavior, however, may be
said to have sprung up largely since the Second World War,
and on premises differing from those that informed the earlier
developments. Although the thinking aspect is not ignored,
and problem-solving continues to be regarded as important—
sometimes under the name of "task"—the present interpretations of group behavior tend to see group members as whole
persons who function in the totality of their selfhood. Distinc-
tions between the "rational" or "thinking" process and "emotional" behavior are seen as having limited, if sometimes prag-

matic, value. The concern for a way of carrying on the common life in a democracy remains, but the spheres in which this democracy is to be realized have been extended beyond the public realm to include areas as diverse as the nuclear family and the corporation executive committee. "Interpersonal relationships" displaces the term "discussion" as a more inclusive designation of the present approach.

These postwar developments are often accredited to the work of Kurt Lewin. Refugee from Nazi Germany, Lewin became founder and director of the Research Center for Group Dynamics at the Massachusetts Institute of Technology, in 1944. His concern was to connect research with action in the field of human behavior. A primary concept was that of field forces operating in group situations to bring about changes in the status of individuals as members of groups. Group atmosphere, levels of reality, group decision, we-feeling, and the like, were terms illustrative of Lewin's thought.[14]

In both its research and its practical implications, Lewin's teaching has been carried further by the movement popularly known as "Group Dynamics." The National Training Laboratories, an affiliate of the National Educational Association, has embodied this development organizationally. "NTL" held its first training laboratory in human relations and group process at Gould Academy, in Bethel, Maine, in 1947. Since then, an expanding program of such laboratories has been held at Bethel and elsewhere, and new designs have been created to meet the needs of a growing range of constituents. Departments and Institutes of Human Relations, Communications, or Behavioral Sciences, as they are variously called, have arisen in many universities, often staffed by social scientists affiliated with "NTL." One phase of the rapid expansion of interest in the field of group dynamics is to be seen in the creation of a wide range of consultative services available to business corporations, educational institutions, volunteer organizations, and religious bodies, for the purpose of improving the interpersonal competence of their officers and staff, as essential to the effective functioning of their structures and the achievement of their goals.

We cannot discuss this expansion further here. Enough may have been said to indicate that knowledge of what takes place in interpersonal groups is now far more detailed, grounded in research, and tested in practice, than many friends or critics of the group movement may suspect. The rapidly accumulating and refined body of research, critically evaluated in experiment and experience, can provide groups with a substantial framework for growth and effective functioning.

A Concern for the Person

3. *Interpersonal groups represent a concern for the person.* The tendencies in our society that make for the depersonalization of people have been remarked frequently by social critics. This depersonalization—which might be called an *in-humanization* of people—can be traced to a number of causes. Prominent among these is the view of the human being to be found among some scientists, best described as *reductionist:* the tendency to reduce the person to a few elementary components and then to claim that this "is all there is to a man." The individual is no longer a human being in his uniqueness and wholeness. He is "economic man," or "psychological man," as in an era of manual labor he was simply a "field *hand.*" In the reductionist view, all aspects of his "complex behavior and intellectual activity will ultimately find satisfactory explanation in terms of the purely physical laws of nature." [15] From this point of view, an anthropologist can describe the idea of the "soul" as a "homeostatic device of purely psychiatric relevance," a "tender-minded misapprehension of the nature of human nature," which is—sad to say—"bad embriology." [16]

There are signs today, however, that such attempts to understand human nature in these reductionary terms may be bad physics, bad psychology, and bad anthropology. Yet enough of this outlook lingers in our intellectual climate to cause many people to ask whether this is all that can be said for human beings. May not an understanding of the person require a point of view inclusive of all the traits, attributes, and characteristics that are essentially human, and a recognition that the category "human being" belongs uniquely to its own class and cannot be reduced to something more elementary, less complex, or—not least—less surrounded with mystery?

A second cause of the trend toward depersonalization of human beings at work today may be summarized in the term, the "technological." The word is used, not in the limited sense of a skill or method of performing some practical operation, but in its more inclusive sense of the whole process by which men are mobilized and used in our society for purposes and in ways that deny their essential humanity. War, even "limited war," is such a denial, and therefore a contradiction of all the goals invoked to justify it. Automation has become the symbol of the disenfranchisement of men from the world of meaningful work, and a sign pointing toward the possible enslavement of human beings to a self-determinative technological process which threatens to take over every aspect of their existence, from the production of goods to the manipulation of genetic inheritance.[17]

Yet a resurgence of concern for the person can be discerned. Some of the symptoms take on a turbulence that may hide their true significance. Unconventional styles of life among some of the younger generation; the violent tone in the arts; rioting in the name of freedom; the insurgence of peoples demanding status as free nations; labor strikes whose real grievance is in the demand to be treated as human beings—all of these express in one way or another the fundamental demand that human persons be valued as human persons. Intuitively, many people today have grasped the import of Harry Stack Sullivan's observation that "most of the ways in which one goes about being a human being could be very different from anything we have ever heard of," [18] and are insisting that we start finding out how and in what measure this possibility can be true for them.

The resurgence of concern for the person expresses itself,

also, in the growing recognition that a man must be understood in terms of his wholeness. Abraham Maslow describes this approach, psychologically, as "holistic, rather than atomistic, functional rather than taxonomic, dynamic rather than static . . . purposive rather than simple-mechanistic." [19] This point of view finds embodiment in such ventures as *The Journal of Creative Behavior*,[20] whose field of inquiry is the development of the creativity, intelligence, and problem-solving ability of human beings; or the Esalen Institute, of Big Sur, California, where advanced processes are created and used for releasing people from inhibiting structures of personality into a larger freedom of self-awareness and a more effective use of capabilities.

Closely allied with such developments as these, and with our interest in interpersonal groups, is the recognition that the individual becomes a person in and through his interpersonal relationships. From infancy on, his growth depends upon the strength, warmth, and richness of his interactions with other significant persons. In his adult years, identification with one or more groups or communities becomes the foundation of his behavior. Ralph Nisbet reports, out of his experience as a personnel officer in the Second World War, that what actually supported the individual soldier was not the indoctrination he was given as to what the war was all about, but his "sense of relatedness to others in his platoon or company." [21] This effective alternative to mass man is not to be found in a recovery of the isolated individual, but in the creation of significant interpersonal relationships within which the personal potentiality of the individual can be nurtured, challenged, and released in its fullness. In our society, such interpersonal relationships are not easily found. Not all small groups can claim to provide them. But at the same time, it may be said that the creation of more significant and more effective interpersonal relationships in primary groups would appear to claim high priority for those persons and institutions concerned for the recovery of the human person in our day.

Value for the Future

4. *Interpersonal groups have high functional value in an open future.* In our culture today, systems of absolute laws, assumptions, values, and beliefs, are dissolving into a worldview which sees the future as relative, tentative, undetermined, and open-ended. Continuous, accelerating change is the only indelible characteristic of that future. In all seriousness we can say today that we do not know where we are going, but we are on our way. Our predicament may not be as perilous as that of the experimental jet pilot who radioed his control tower, "I'm lost, but I'm making record time!" But we are already far out from the old perdurable landscapes where we could always take a fix and establish our location.

Commonplace as these observations have become, we have not yet grasped their radical implications. In almost all of human history men have been able to take for granted the immutability of some system of absolutes. The "ontocratic" patterns of civilization saw every aspect of society—government, art, economy, religion—as fixed within a cosmic design that was total and absolute. The function of king and state was to give form to this cosmic design in the human domain, as the function of religion was to celebrate the cosmic order of all things, and thereby to sanctify the human order. Christianity, on the other hand, when it has been true to its Biblical origins, has insisted that the static cosmic orders have been overthrown by the God who himself creates freely, and who bestows on men the privilege of participating in His creation, and the responsibility for their own future.[22]

The shift from absolutes to the tentative, dynamic outlook can be illustrated in the scientific attitude. In its earlier phases, science was assumed to be based upon "laws," which—though they were sometimes little more than shrewd guesses, or a mixture of fact and fancy—were sometimes held to prove the inexorable, deterministic character of all things, including human existence. Traces of this attitude can be found in the dogmatic tone used by the reductionists, described earlier.

Others found in the laws of science a proof of a divine, in-scrutable Will that created (though it might no longer govern) all things.

But scientists today are content to make only proximate statements describing or summarizing the probabilities they discern. The laws of today become the rejects of tomorrow. The consequences of this change in outlook are both funda-mental and practical. For one thing, they call in question the whole metaphysical basis upon which the absolutes of the past were grounded. As Leslie Dewart has shown, the structure of Roman Catholicism, in both its theology and its institu-tional order, rests upon Greek metaphysics in which absolute, hierarchical orders are implicit. The Protestant Reformation did not question that kind of metaphysical basis; it only sought to return the church to a purer form of orders and absolutes. Today, Dewart insists, theology must be content with a "rela-tive" rather than an "absolute" theism, or doctrine of God, and must work with "developmental dogma" rather than fixed and immutable systems of doctrine.[23] The newer scientific out-look is responsible in a large measure for this radical change in theological outlook. At the same time, the scientific outlook itself is in large measure possible as a consequence of a Chris-tian understanding of God as One who deposes all fixed cosmic powers and initiates an order of freedom, responsibility, and creativity in which He calls men to participate.

If our discussion thus far has seemed unnecessarily abstruse, we can quickly recall concrete ways in which our understand-ing of faith and our day-by-day religious behavior is affected. Fewer and fewer people today feel that they can speak with absolute conviction about what they believe or believe in. A campus minister asks how students shall think of themselves as "Christian" when they are not able to say what they believe, and when they feel that such ways of confident speaking are not now, and probably never will be, open to them. Or again, who is able to say with authority what actions are always right, always wrong? Such radical shifts from the absolute to the rela-tive, from the fixed to the tentative, from the stable to the dynamic, can be seen in a wide span of attitudes, beliefs, and assumptions that direct our lives today.

Against the background of this shift, how is the function of interpersonal groups to be described? The temptation would be to claim for such groups the power to answer all the questions that arise out of this new situation. Yet some strategic functions for interpersonal groups in an open-ended culture can be suggested. If creativity in theoretical science is becoming more and more a function of groups of scientists and less and less the activity of the solitary genius, the same process may be assumed to have its use in the formation of a new and relevant religious understanding. Still further, if theology arises out of reflection upon experience, understood in faith, a fresh and vital emergence of theology may wait for the contributions that might be made by lay men and women, as they describe and reflect upon the implications of their living experience.[24]

The same process can contribute to the creation of a "new," and renewing, morality. The complementarity and mutual correction proposed by Professor Long would seem to require a means for continuing exchange of views and insights between persons involved in the ethical problems that confront men in our world.

All of this means replacing the voice of authority, speaking solo from above, with the rise and fall of many voices in animated interchange, questioning, criticizing, encouraging, confessing, and accepting, as an accompaniment to their actual involvement in the ethical and moral quandaries of existence. In this process, interpersonal groups in some form can make an indispensable contribution.

But while this process is taking form and is spread through our society, there is a corollary function for interpersonal groups that should not be overlooked. In a time when old foundations are eroding and old assurances are dissolving, the alternative to drift and despair will be found in the kind of human anchorage where persons can find security, strength, and orientation for life as they must live it. People need *homes;* and the homes of the future will be found, not in fixed systems or structures, but in clusters and nuclei of persons in relations. "Someday you'll have a new home," said the social worker to the boy in the refugee camp. "We already have a home," he retorted. "All we need is a place to put it." As our society becomes increasingly transient in every respect, with more and more people in it becoming refugees dispossessed of their old fixed abodes, interpersonal groups may provide the stabilities of a home within which are nurtured new insights for faith, new moral valuing, and new courage to direct the processes of continuing change into more appropriate, humane fulfillments.

Total Communication

5. *Interpersonal groups provide for "total communication."* Recent developments in our understanding of communication and social interaction give a new emphasis to a primary characteristic of interpersonal groups. This can be described by such terms as "total" or "immediate" or "wholly present" communication. Its pattern may be "nonsequential" as contrasted with rationally ordered development of ideas, and the relationships taking place may be described by words like "participative" or "in depth encountering." Terms such as these and the ideas they suggest have been popularized in the writings of Marshall McLuhan, but they are not confined to his works alone.

McLuhan's argument, stated too briefly and too simply, is that up until now modern society has been organized by the "linear" sequence of the printed page. Reading a book must be done line by line, page by page (although attempts have been made to teach children to read in larger units of perception). The consequence of this linear style has been to give dominance to the rational, logical ordering of concepts, and to put a premium upon the detached, noninvolved attitude on the part of a reader, and upon our basic ways of carrying on interpersonal relationship.

In a study of a large research corporation, Professor Chris Argyris, of Yale, discovered what he calls the "pyramidal values" that governed the relationships among top executives.

> . . . Pyramidal organizations imply a strategy of effective human relationships. This rational strategy emphasizes (1) the centrality of organizational objectives, (2) the suppression of relevant feelings and the emphasis upon intellective, cognitive thinking, and (3) the use of power and control to obtain the compliance of the participants.[25]

Only with great difficulty were these executives able to see how these values tended to sterilize and make frustrating the work they and their subordinates were trying to carry on. Communication was stifled, mistrust increased, creativity gave way to "playing it safe," and the conditions for basic, creative research were destroyed. McLuhan's argument would suggest that this is the inevitable outcome of the style of relationships that have grown up in our linearly oriented society.

Electronic communication, especially as instrumented through television, is changing all of that. Encounter becomes instantaneous, inclusive, and involving of the whole person. "We are suddenly eager to have people declare their beings totally." Because electronic communication is really an extension of our nervous systems, it "favors the inclusive and participational spoken word over the specialist written word," or, for that matter, the monological lecture or sermon. These are displaced by dialogue which gives "a relation in depth, and without delegation of function and powers." Electronic technology is creating a culture in which "we must all interact and react, using all of our faculties at once." [26]

Critics of McLuhan's thesis ask whether he goes too far and lacks sufficient supporting evidence for the claims he makes. But signs of his accuracy in explaining some social behavior in today's society are not wanting. Advertising begins to take on the "cool" characteristics that he describes, and to stress the *"right now"* quality of a product. On campuses, students revolt against the rationalized, specialized, "linear" curriculum, and the nonparticipative patterns of an educational process built upon the monological lecture and the printed page of the textbook. TV programs now and then shift their design from the linear narrative of the western or the beads-on-a-string of old-style variety acts to a mosaic in which song, dance, act, move in and out to form a visual and aural montage. And who listens any more to the public address, whether of politician, statesman, or pulpiteer, as though this monologue were an event of compelling power and importance?

We must wait a little longer, perhaps, to see how the developments in communication, described by McLuhan and others, will affect the functioning of interpersonal groups. Without question, much of the information about what goes on in interpersonal groups which we now have will be found to correlate readily and fully with the implications of this new understanding of "instant communication" and "whole-person participation." But at least one implication already becomes clear: interpersonal groups can no longer be designed and carried on as though they were simply a new framework within which the older linear, rationalistic patterns of intercourse can be continued.

This subversion has been the particular temptation of church programmers who are preoccupied with a didactic approach in their efforts to "communicate the Gospel" or to give "theological competence" to the so-called "illiterate" layman. A recent plan for "action Bible study" illustrates this temptation. The stated purpose of the plan would seem to be aware of some of the point of view suggested by McLuhan. The process aims at getting everyone into the act and at fostering a climate of search, openness, and passionate engagement. It seeks to evoke "Biblical images" rather than to extract Biblical ideas. Yet the design for a group meeting neatly programs the group's progress through four main phases of discussion, with a time schedule indicating the number of minutes to be spent on each phase! "Total," "participative," "whole-person interacting" group functioning can never be confined, scheduled, and directed in such linear, rationalistic ways as this.

This warning was verified in another denominational program. "House-groups" were set up to provide a framework for briefing church members on the denomination's mission program. Members were recruited on a neighborhood basis, to meet in homes for four bi-weekly meetings. The program for each session was carefully spelled out in the manual. A later study of over a hundred of these groups revealed that many of them died before the series of four meetings had been held. But some groups threw out the syllabus at their first meeting, and instead of being briefed on missions, dived into their own needs and problems. A number of these groups continued to meet regularly far beyond the four-session schedule originally planned. A somewhat similar outcome took place among groups in the National Council of Churches, "Project Laity," described by Dr. Thomas Bennett in a later chapter of this book.

In the society taking shape in our day, it would seem safe to say that modern, participative man will no longer be content with the options now offered him in many of his social relationships, whether in educational institutions, business corporations, political parties, or religious bodies. He is no longer content to be a passive spectator, sitting in the crowd, the classroom, the staff meeting, or the congregation. Nor—we may hope—will he be content to escape from this submissiveness into the private mesmerizing world of television. He will seek those relationships, groupings, and arenas where participative, depth interaction, is open to him at every level of his need and aspiration as a complete human being.

Interpersonal groups, in the wide diversity and the new dimensions described in the chapters of this book, may provide—or may be capable of providing—the kind of scene and relationship he seeks. What can take place in such groups must be described not as a discussion or an argument, or a learning effort, or even a "worship experience" in the way that phrase has degenerately come to be used. It can be suggested only by that marvelous new term (old term made new by new use) given us by a generation raised upon an electronic instantaneity—a true *"happening."*

In the chapters that follow, the five tendencies we have been summarizing here will be seen, in various proportions and mixtures. They do not attempt to describe what has been known through experience by cutting and cramming it into a framework such as our five points might impose. What they aim to do is to write about that experience "as it is"—which is always richer in meaning than any systematic scheme can provide.

2. A Home for Persons

THOMAS M. STEEN

The Reverend Thomas M. Steen is minister of the First Methodist Church in Corning, New York. The story of his first experience with groups in a church is given in Chapter I of *Spiritual Renewal Through Personal Groups*. In Corning, his ministry through groups has grown in depth and consequence, and he is widely sought as leader and consultant in the group movement both here and abroad. This chapter offers an account of his basic philosophy for group life, illustrated out of his rich experience.

Ten years ago I was concerned with trying to find a way whereby the church could be renewed. I was anxious that she might once again become the channel of God's grace, that she might free men to discover their uniqueness in God. If this happened, such men would use the church as a laboratory to test their newly discovered insights, and renewal would be a natural by-product. My own intense interest was often responsible for pushing people in the direction of renewal and protecting them from church structures that might discourage them or put out their new flame of love for God and the church. I am certain that I helped to erect a roadblock against true renewal both for myself and for those in research groups.

Several years ago I read Frank Laubach's religious classic *Letters By A Modern Mystic*, which is composed of letters written home during a period in his life when he was assailed by doubts and discouragement. Having served for a number of years as a missionary to the Moros in the Philippines, he became aware that his enthusiasm and love for life were gradually drying up. During these days of anguish as he wrestled with despair and loneliness, he kept a diary of his thoughts and feelings. One evening as he sat on Signal Hill reveling in the awesome beauty of the sunset, he heard God speak to him, "The most beautiful thing in the universe for you is Lanao stretching around the lake at your feet for it contains the beauty of immense need. You must awaken hunger there for until they hunger they cannot be fed."

Is this not the key for which we have been searching? In the church we have offered to do everything to save men from their fears and anxieties. We have preached to them—offering Christ as a way of life, offering them religious work, and inoculated them with Biblical and religious teaching. To what end and for what purpose? Have we religious leaders understood Jesus when he said "The Kingdom of God is in you"? Is it not our task to awaken the ultimate hunger and thirst that God has hidden in every life? Assuming that this is our job, how do we awaken this hunger so that man can begin the journey of discovering his uniqueness and authenticity as a person?

Community in Transition

After working intimately with groups in one church for ten years, I moved to Corning, New York, a community caught in transition. Once a railroad town, it now is gradually becoming one of the great centers of glass research, bringing in hundreds of men trained in the physical sciences. The majority of these newcomers are younger men whose families want the conveniences and opportunities offered in a large metropolitan center. So, as happens in many American communities, a tug of war began between the older citizens and the new employees who knew nothing of the community's past. They wanted improved library facilities, a top-notch school system, and every modern convenience promised by an affluent society.

In the center of this social change stood the church. What was her role to be? How could she bridge the gap between those who revered religious tradition and those of the younger

generation who couldn't care less for the past? Concerned as
I was that there must be a renewed church in the heart of the
community, meeting people where they live and ministering
to them on that level, where could I begin?

There was only one place to begin—with people in their own
experience. This approach is the long way around. It does not
produce miracles overnight. It assumes that one must find a
way to initiate the new even while holding on to the traditions
of the past. One does not impose a program of renewal on any
people, nor does he fight the old order. Renewal will come
when there is an equal hunger and thirst for authenticity on
the part of a minister. Unless he is thoroughly convinced that
this can happen, he will be swallowed up in the old forms,
trapped in the traditional structures to which men cling for
security.

The committee that interviewed me had been meeting for
several months as they made a careful appraisal of the future
of First Church. In their continuing study, many experienced
for the first time a feeling of community. It was no problem,
therefore, to convince them that they should continue their
quest as I now joined them. We met regularly to discuss what
our common ministry was to those inside the church as well as
to those outside. If this experience of being in community was
really the church, how could it be extended? They said that
they were actually listening to other points of view, that they
were learning to confront their anxieties rather than hide from
them. Where before they had spoken rather guardedly about
what they believed and felt, they were now discovering a freedom to speak openly and honestly about the things that were
of the utmost importance. This was the beginning of an entirely new concept of the church. What they studied, projected,
and shared was meaningful and enjoyable, and caused the
church to move out in new directions.

Our first step was to find a way to make Christian education
come alive. In a school of learning we said it was as important,
if not more important, to learn an experience openness of
mind and heart and honesty in dealing with one's life as it was

to learn religious facts. We insisted that it was as essential to
come to know the person we taught as it was to know his name.
Where did we ever get the idea that we are to instruct others
in the way of life and at the same time have no honest relationships with these same persons? Our instruction in the
Protestant Church for the most part has often been formal,
cold, impersonal, given to a discussing of values which the
leader has no intention of adopting for himself. It has been
my observation that when young people and adults actually
experience openness in small groups, they become the best
teachers. Education that leads to spiritual growth must be
shared in such a way that facts and feeling for the facts are
fused together.

I suggested that the committee might make a study of the
Church of the Saviour in Washington, D.C., which was experimenting in this kind of learning process. Those who wished to
join the church must meet a certain disciplined standard before being received into membership. Since many church members are religiously illiterate and spiritually undisciplined, the
Church of the Saviour requires prospective new members to
join a class studying the Bible, the history of the Church, the
mission of the modern church, and the nature of spiritual
disciplines. The class meets twice a week for a period from one
to two years. When a person requests membership in the
church, he is asked to contribute 10 per cent of his income and
to accept some responsibility for mission either in the church
or the community. Even after they have become members, they
must join a disciplined group for learning and sharing. This
small church (approximately seventy-five members) has accepted a mission to reach the unchurched by sponsoring a
coffee house and a Potter's House where young adults can learn
to express their religious convictions and feelings in the fine
arts. Since many from the congregation of First Church were
employed in the Corning Glass Works and often went to
Washington on business, they were encouraged to visit both
the church and the Potter's House.

In the meantime, I invited Gordon Cosby to come to First

Church to present a series of three lectures on "The Christian Faith—A Disciplined Way of Life." The committee encouraged all who attended to be present for all three lectures, so that those who were ready for participation in depth groups could hear the complete story. Approximately one hundred forty-five people registered and attended. Realizing that many people respond emotionally to a new venture but are unprepared to pay a price for being part of a disciplined group, certain follow-up meetings were scheduled. At the close of the lectures it was announced that arrangements had been made to play the taped lectures on three successive Monday evenings. Forty-five persons attended the first evening and finally twenty-two responded at the close of the third session saying they were ready for the experience of joining a disciplined research group. As they met together they made only one stipulation, that those who joined should agree to come into the group for one year.

A Concern for the Person

The first several weeks were given to discovering who they were as persons and then attempting to understand what they actually were looking for. Such questions as the following were raised: What does it mean to be an authentic person? What are the resources for such a study? How does a person become his true self? They often found that they were at cross purposes with each other, and they had difficulty in determining where they should begin. One member indicated that he wanted to read and study one of the Gospels—this had been a long-time desire of his, and now his group presented an opportunity for him to carry out his plan. He urged the others to go along with him. He soon discovered that they were unwilling to commit themselves for they, too, had their own ideas of what they wanted to do. It took all of them some time to understand that a research group was not something anyone could use for his own purpose. They still had to learn that a disciplined group was "a home" where the members give themselves to listening in an attempt to understand what others are desperately trying to say. They were looking for a common ground where they could begin their search. Frustration and tension grew those first few weeks as they sought to be a group in spirit as well as in name.

Renewal must begin with a concern for the person, not the church. To use a disciplined group so that new life may emerge and change the church is to use people and defeat the purpose of renewal. If participating members can come to see themselves as channels for God's love, if they can take the truth discovered with the mind and through discipline cause this truth to come alive in them as persons, then renewal is on its way. Dynamic power will flow from such disciplined members to all the structures of our culture, including the Christian church.

Fifteen years ago when I first began working with the groups, those who participated were mostly interested in finding a way to believe in a personal God. Having been brought up in a world where the church was often separated from the world, they could not find God in their daily life. In those few intervening years, however, our culture has grown more concerned with man—not God. Men and women are looking for a direction that will lead to meaning. They are far from certain that it is God who imparts meaning to their lives, and they do not know where to begin the search. Dr. Paul Tournier of Switzerland is one writer who has helped them the most. His books *The Meaning of Persons* and *The Healing of Persons* have stimulated them perhaps more than any other modern writer.

As they learned to be more trusting in their relationships, they found the freedom to set up guidelines for their bi-weekly sessions. After the exhilarating, free-wheeling experience of simply talking at each other, they gradually came to realize that they knew what each other thought about most subjects. Even this new freedom of doing exactly what they wanted to do led to boredom. So, certain principles of procedure were adopted. (1) To meet every two weeks at a given hour and to be present at these sessions unless they were ill or out of the city. (2) To read Paul Tournier's book, *The Meaning of Persons*. (3) To be consciously aware of differences in their response and to learn how to deal honestly with any statement of fact, insight, or feeling, including their own feelings. (4) To determine what they could do with this newly discovered truth, for truth accepted only with the mind is but the first step toward experiencing the ultimate truth as a person.

The formation of these guidelines was crucial, for it indicated that they were moving from the discussion state to the point where they must act out the truth as they had come to know it. Only in doing the truth, acting it out as one knows it, can one come to discover his own authenticity as a person and, at the same time, experience God as fact. When this first lesson has been learned, every beginner has at last set his feet on the road to becoming an authentic person.

In the meantime, a new spirit was being felt at the very heart of the church, a spirit that fed and nourished people in the process of questioning and exploring. As the Pastoral Relations Committee began to deal with the live issues of the total community, their new enthusiasm began to spread. They were not thinking of renewal in the sense of creating new structures for the sake of structures. They were attempting to open up channels in a city church which had given little or no thought to the subject of renewal. The committee had the traditional expectancy that a new minister would of himself bring new life into the church. As they worked on their agenda they came through to the insight as to what the term "ministry" meant. They were now ready for experimentation, and what they did supported and undergirded the questing in the small research groups.

Free to Explore

If the church is to be made new, there must be freedom for persons to explore and try out new approaches. In one of the original groups the members began to share the real joy of worshipping together—in fact, they found such meaning that they were tempted to give up the Sunday worship which they said was dull and obsolete. They also became aware of the fact that many of their friends never attended church services. Finally, they recommended to the adult council in Christian education that a course be conducted on the meaning and relevance of worship in a secular culture.

Such a course was developed with the assistance of Dr. Jack Lewis, director of the United Religious Work at Cornell University and formerly director of the Faith and Life Student Program at Austin, Texas. He helped them to see that the more traditional service, with its familiar prayers, creeds, hymns, and liturgical pattern, met the needs of some but did not reach many of the young adults. So, after a number of weeks exploring the history of worship, they sent a recommendation to the official board that beginning in the fall season two services of worship should be conducted, the first to experiment with new forms of worship, and the second to carry on the traditional pattern.

A pamphlet suggesting guidelines for participation in both services was sent to each church family. In part it said:

1. Worship, both private and corporate, must be entered into regularly.
2. Worship is not a spectator sport. It is a participation event. Each person's contribution in singing, prayer, sharing, is important.
3. Worship needs preparation. It demands one's attention, and one needs to prepare himself emotionally and intellectually for the experience.
4. The services of worship at 9:00 and 11:10 are planned to meet different needs. If one feels that the format or means of expression of one service will be offensive to him, it is suggested that he attend that service which will serve as a channel for his response to God. Worship is not a *smorgasbord* to be sampled; it is an experience to be entered into.
5. Worship is for the person with the open mind—prepared to be confronted by God. It is not for the person who wants to argue over the order and expression of a particular service.

What happened in the following year was really tremendous. Congregation and staff alike learned many new things—things that kept us constantly changing both our conduct and content of worship. We initiated a practice period of ten minutes before the early service when instruction in worship could be given, new hymns learned (members were encouraged to write new words for old hymn tunes). This was the period when the ministers had fun in working with the congregation as we prepared ourselves for the experience that was to follow. The congregation (not the choir) opened the service with the Call to Worship. The children and youth choirs were moved from the choir loft to a place immediately in front of the congregation so that there was a more closely knit relationship. Often the congregation sang certain parts of an anthem or hymn with the choirs. The minister delivered his sermon from the floor level of the congregation (the pulpit has seldom been used in this service). The ministers and laymen participate in dialogical sermons, and excerpts from secular plays are presented. The congregation pronounces the benediction upon each other as they turn toward the center aisle of the church, and they conclude the service with the singing of the traditional "Amen." The secret of its growth was in its informal nature, the period of preparation, and the active participation of many in the actual conduct of the service. The fun and the joy experienced in the practice period were carried over into the service itself. As one twelve-year-old youngster said, "Gee, I never knew worship could be so much fun."

Self-Confrontation

The groups become the place where a member comes to grips with the major issues of his life and confronts his real self. On one occasion a member came to me and said, "I've decided to leave the group." "Why?" I asked. Then she replied, "I can see where this experience has taken me and I have no intention of following through. I do not wish to change my life." So I said, "You'll be back." She replied laughingly, "How do

you know so much?" I said, "Once a person has experienced
the reality of looking into his own life and discovering what
he might become, he will be restless until he returns to the
search and confrontation." She did leave the group and later
in the year returned with her husband to become members of
the Couples group. Several months afterwards they returned
again and she said, "My husband and I are leaving. We had
many differences of opinion before we were members, and now
we discover that we have twice as many differences." What she
said was undoubtedly true, for this happens with many couples
as they seek a deeper level of commitment and meaning in
their marriage. The groups do, however, provide an atmosphere of love, trust, and honesty where persons may learn
something new about their partners in marriage, can accept
what they find, and free the other one to grow in his uniqueness, into his true self.

After several years in Corning, I invited to our home these
research groups as well as those who desired to learn what actually happens in such groups. They were asked to share with
each other values they found in belonging. Some of the more
typical statements were: "The group compels me to study so
that I am beginning to know what I believe." "I need a discipline for my prayer life—I simply cannot pray alone." "I begin
to see myself—my real needs, my weaknesses and my strengths
in a new light—and I find that I can accept myself for what I
am." "Thursday is a different day because I spend the first few
hours with men in a common search." Most of them said that
the group was a place where they could be at home. One member said, "I can give up any other activity, but I certainly cannot give up my research group. Here is a place where I feel at
home, where I can freely express what I think and know that
I will be accepted." "Here is the place where I am stimulated
and encouraged to go out in new directions, where I can discover a depth of meaning I never knew before." In this world
of transition where all values seem to be questioned and there
is constant change, the group becomes a home for the growth
of persons.

3. Interpersonal Groups and the Church

Are interpersonal groups peripheral to the life of the church?
Recent concentration on group dynamics has led some to see
groups as secular or humanistic developments, lacking roots
in church tradition or faith. In this chapter, Dr. Wedel shows
how group life is deeply and centrally embedded in the Christian community and its faith as described in the New Testament. Honorary Canon and Warden Emeritus of the College
of Preachers, Washington Cathedral, Dr. Wedel has taught
in universities and seminaries. His writings include *The Coming Great Church,* and the Exposition of the Epistle to the
Ephesians in *The Interpreter's Bible.* He was one of the
earliest leaders of the movement to develop group dynamics
training for the Episcopal Church.

"This was the greatest religious experience of my life." This
confession, repeatedly voiced during an evaluation session at
the close of a Group Development, or "Group Dynamics,"
Laboratory at Bethel, Maine, which I was privileged to attend,
came as a shock to a number of Laboratory members who, like
myself, represented church interests. Redemptive experience
in Christian fellowship—is this not one of the most essential
marks of what the very word "church" should mean when it
manifests such basic New Testament images of the church as
Body of Christ and Fellowship of the Holy Spirit? Has something gone wrong when large numbers of institutionally loyal
church members are given their first introduction to a genuine
interpersonal fellowship experience, on a level of conscious

Rev. Frank E. Brainard
Collinwood U. M. Ch.
15232 St. Clair Ave.

Clyde Huther
  Box 2457
  Whitehouse, Ohio 43571

Peggy Vance
3 South Street
Leipsic, Ohio

Mrs. William Collins
    (Alice)
8 7 Leming Rd.
Hanover, Penna.

L Imler
532 W. 4th
Chillicothe, O.   45601

Jane Meyers
5885 Sinclair Road
Columbus, Ohio 43224

Mrs. George C. McLaren

George
140 Featsworth Dr
Chillicothe Ohio

Ruth S. Tompkins
411 Spring Ave.
Pomeroy, O. 45769

Mrs. Irma Patchen
13425 La Plaisance Wds
La Salle Mich 48145

Mrs. Daisie F. Wells
127 Locust St.
Huntington, W. Va. 25705

Mrs. Florence Conine
120 West Elm St Deshler Ohio
43516

Martha Bower
1416 Chesterton Sq. N.
Columbus, Ohio 43224

participation at least, in a secular group outside church anchorage? Instead of church leadership being compelled to a humiliating salute to secular social science for insight into what interpersonal fellowship means, should not the relationship of pupil and teacher have been the very reverse of this—social scientists finding in the common life of the church a primary model for their exploration of what interpersonal group life symbolizes in creating a humanized social order?

Yet the twentieth century is not the first era in church history which illustrates the truth of the word of Jesus: "The sons of this world are wiser in their own generation than the sons of light" (Luke 16:8).

One of the first results of an honest self-appraisal of our communal life in our churches is to admit that the New Testament images of the church place us under judgment. John Wesley, a pioneer in personal groups, indicted the church of his time:

> Christian fellowship, where is it to be found? Look east or west, north or south; name what parish you please: Is this Christian fellowship there? Rather, are not the bulk of parishioners a mere rope of sand? What Christian connection is there between them? What intercourse in spiritual things? What watching over each other's soul? What bearing of one another's burdens? [1]

Since it is always easier to see the mote in a brother's eye than the beam in one's own eye, Protestant observers of Roman Catholic church life frequently have little difficulty in seeing the neglect of the fellowship mark of the church in the Catholic tradition, though the recent laity and liturgical renewal movements in Catholicism are inaugurating notable changes. It is not surprising, therefore, that a leading Catholic "renewal theologian" like Yves Congar, whose *Lay People in the Church* boldly pleads for a rediscovery of the church as the whole people of God, finds in some of our Protestant renewal movements models for indicting Catholic neglect of Christian fellowship as an essential mark of the church.

The profound mystery of the church in its wholeness has, to cite Fr. Congar,

... often been rediscovered by being lived from below, in small groups that found the Church in her fullness through little Church cells, in whose constitution the religious subject was personally and communally active. It is not surprising that, seeing these new forms of Church life, plenty of good Catholics have exclaimed, "This is Protestant!" There is, of course, nothing Protestant about it. It is simply a taking back into possession and use that aspect of the Church which Protestantism developed onesidedly.[2]

If we replace the word "sacerdotalism" with its cognate word "clericalism," indictments of a lack of Christian fellowship witness such as those cited by our Catholic brethren and a John Wesley can apply to our contemporary state also. Fr. Congar confronts us with the observation that "Protestant communions, starting from strict congregational premises and an associational community basis, are in practice almost as clericalised as the Catholic Church."[3] One of the most competent recent appraisals of present-day Protestant polity validates Fr. Congar's observation: "For many Protestants the ministry is very nearly the whole of the church, and the minister is the 'preacher.' Such an overemphasis on preaching and the personality of the preacher entailed the neglect of other aspects of the ministry and other phases of the work of the Church." The author, Robert Michaelsen, pleads for "a rediscovery of the ecclesia of the Scriptures."[4]

Two Marks of the Church—Institution and Fellowship

Leaving aside the ministry of the parish house with its proliferations (which deserves an analysis on its own), it is surely a fact that multitudes of Protestant Church members experience what "church" means in their lives as one concentrated on attendance at a church service which does not demand any personal participation except that of listening to an address called a sermon or partaking as lone individuals of the bread and wine in a communion service. The worshipper, to be sure, may join in the singing of a hymn and may greet the minister at the church door. He can, however, avoid the ministry of the

coffee hour (not to be belittled as a halfway station to interpersonal group experience). Of the two great commandments
of the Gospel, he may have been moved to greater submission
of conscience to the first in his private Christian life, but, if
love of neighbor is placed alongside the first commandment,
he can escape a "now" token of obedience. For loving one's
neighbor, there must first be a neighbor, and "neighbor" must
mean more than the physical presence of an anonymous fellow occupant of a pew. The worshipper may, accordingly, himself remain "anonymous"—"without a name," as the dictionary
defines the word.

Before the norm of the *ecclesia* of the New Testament is
brought into the discussion, however, a word of caution in
concentrating on indictments of the church's institutional life,
whether Catholic or Protestant, is in order. How easy it is to
fall victim to a false alternative! The church as institution
does have a mission to perform in its own right, a mission to
which Catholicism has been, in its turn, a faithful witness. No
image of the church is probably more important for our small
group evangelism than the one given us in the twentieth verse
of Matthew 18: "Where two or three are gathered together,
there am I in the midst of them." *Ubi Christus, ibi ecclesia.* Let
even the smallest cell group of Christian believers, accordingly,
rejoice in the fact that it can enjoy a presence of Christ equal,
or possibly superior to, that of a cathedral congregation num-
bering thousands of worshippers. But the "two or three," however perfectly an incarnation of oneness in Christ, cannot itself
have created the Gospel message of salvation. And to avoid
some form of institutional empowering of such Gospel proclamation is a historical impossibility.

When all correctives against false alternatives have received
full attention, it nevertheless remains a fact that the mark of
the church as Christian fellowship is the most obvious blank
in the average Christian's experience of "church." It is a
strange blank even in the classic Reformation confessional definition of the church as a congregation "in which the pure

Word of God is preached and the Sacraments be adminis-
tered." Back to Scripture, then!

Back to Holy Scripture!

A full marshaling of Biblical proof texts for highlighting the
mark of the church as a fellowship cannot be ventured here.
Almost the whole Bible could be a massive proof text. Emil
Brunner's *The Misunderstanding of the Church*,[5] one-sided
as it may be, furnishes heavy artillery in defense of such a
conclusion. Modern individualist pietism is simply not Biblical. We have somehow equated "personal" with "individualist" religion. The very concept of person, rightly appre-
hended, implies membership in a community. "No personal
being," Paul Tillich reminds us, "exists without communal
being. There is no person without encounter with other persons. Persons can grow only in the communion of personal
encounter." [6]

Personal encounter, interpersonal brotherliness, mutual love
among fellow members—the church in the New Testament
takes these for granted as essential marks of its very existence.
The image of the church as Body of Christ, for example, implies the presence within it of "many made one," each member
a person in his own right, but still a member-in-community.
Entire chapters in St. Paul's letters spell this out. Jesus addressed the disciple-group with the salutation "You are all
brethren" (Matthew 23:8). The images of the family and of the
household are so frequent in the New Testament picture of the
early church that a concordance is needed to list all the proof
passages. The "house-church," which is a novelty for us, was
practically the norm for early Christianity. (See Romans 16:5
and Philemon 2 for typical allusions.) In the opening chapters
of the Acts of the Apostles we note such phrases as "all together
in one place" (2:1) and "those who believed were of one heart
and soul" (4:32). Climactic for a picture of interpersonal relatedness is the great "church chapter" in the Epistle to the
Ephesians—Chapter 4—with its matchless appeals for communal

group unity. Even the most successful Group Dynamics Laboratory triumphs in creating interpersonal maturity are still foothill exemplars of what group dynamism can achieve when it takes form in a truly Christian fellowship. Would any human relations scientist, with only humanistic motivations at his disposal, dream of setting forth as an attainable goal an interpersonal group life such as the one which the author of Ephesians pictures as norm for the church? "Let all bitterness and wrath and clamor and slander," so reads his climactic appeal (4:31 and 32), "be put away from you, with all malice, and be kind to one another, tenderhearted, forgiving one another, as God in Christ forgave you."

When, accordingly, all due tribute is paid by the fellowship evangelism of the churches to our human relations scientists for their help in discerning the therapeutic power of even a purely secular group, Christian fellowship can lay claim to a *plus* of such power. "If you who are only social scientists," so a paraphrase of a familiar verse of the New Testament (Matthew 7:11) might read, "know how to explore and then give guidance for utilizing the dynamics of a group for the humanization of relationships between man and man in our common life, *how much more* can the Fellowship of the Holy Spirit, when truly manifested, exhibit this power of social grace!"

But the light thrown by the New Testament on the evangelizing ministry of Christian fellowship is not limited to texts which describe the church and her interpersonal life directly and as such. Possibly on an even deeper level the Gospel message of reconciliation between God and man and then between man and man can itself yield profound insights for this ministry. St. Paul in his Epistles chose for a central clue to that Gospel message the symbol of justification by faith, or, in more complete phrasing, justification by grace through faith (Romans 3:20; Ephesians 2:8). An average congregation today may well be puzzled not only by the very word "justification" itself but even more by a claim that this has profound relevance for its fellowship life.

Yet the human need which St. Paul has in mind as backdrop

for his proclamation of justification by grace, so Rudolf Bult-mann suggests, is simply what we call today the *"need for recognition."* This need "belongs to every man, and is already noticeable in children, and can assume the most varied forms." *"Man cannot exist at all without recognition,* without being recognized by others, without rejoicing in recognition him-self. . . . But it is a fundamental misconception for him to think that he can extract recognition and establish his claim for recognition through what he does—through his work in-stead of his being." Hence St. Paul's contrast between justifica-tion by works and justification by grace.

To clarify this contrast Bultmann employs the analogy of a person entering into a relationship of genuine friendship or love. "He knows that he does not bring about his friendship or his love as a 'work' by virtue of which he gains the friend-ship or love of the other party, but that the other party in returning it is just as free as he is himself, and that he can only bestow his friendship or his love as a gift." [7]

Social Science—Its Value and Its Limitations

Now, with this clue to the problem of interpersonal relation-ships kept in mind, turn to what happens in a group experi-ence—*any* group, to begin with, even a teen-age gang unified by nothing more than an *esprit de corps* dedicated to vandal-ism! An exception may have to be made for groups under purely authoritarian or *laissez faire* leadership. A minimum of member freedom is essential. But, granted the presence of the latter, every group is an arena for testing the two contrasted pathways to recognition—by works or by grace. To illustrate the latter first, in any cohesive group tokens of experiencing recognition as a gift inevitably appear.

The individual is addressed by name and receives the dignity of participation in dialogue. He is listened to. He is asked to accept a role serving the group's goal, with resultant self-awareness of his capabilities and limitations (compare St. Paul's allusions to "diversity of gifts": I Corinthians 12:4–6). He ex-

periences the power resident in the group of acceptance and
rejection—the latter on occasion so traumatic that it is equivalent to a death sentence even when no literal execution is con-
templated. (There are instances of college students committing
suicide on failing fraternity election.)

All these powers have received acute analysis by our human
relations scientists. I doubt, however, whether they have given
equal attention to the other pathway to personal recognition—
that of "works." Graduates of Group Life Laboratories normally testify to the therapeutic benefits they have received
from their group participation. But the demonic and destructive
elements in interpersonal relationships have frequently been
veiled in such a protected setting and not permitted to exhibit
their full potential. But these are also present in all group life,
a Christian fellowship not excepted.

We can think of the rivalry for leadership in even the most
democratically conducted group, or the continuous battle,
often hidden from view, for attention. "Who shall speak first?"
"Which of my many 'selves' shall I open to group inspection?"
"Which mask shall I wear to make a good impression, even if
this be the mask of humility?" "I am grateful for being accepted by the group, but I wonder whether this extends beyond acceptance of the usefulness in pursuit of the group's goal
of one or more of my talents or career achievements; the deep
hunger for love of my 'being' and not my 'works' is still unsatis-
fied." "Although I admire my neighbor in the group and
salute his talents, envy and jealousy still poison my interpersonal relationship with him; in fact, I experience loneliness
here more painfully than in solitude." (One could recall
Sartre's bitter line in his *No Exit:* "Hell is other people," and
his picture of the characters in the drama as having no eyelids.)

Questions and confessions like these could proliferate. They
contain a warning that to idealize the power of group democracy for solving our human relationship problems in their
deeper and hidden dimensions under the guidance of the insights of social science alone is dangerous. A critic of group
dynamics theory from the point of view of theological insights

accuses it of "naïve optimism concerning the nature of man and the power of reason alone to alter human relationships." Its demands "are impossible without the empowering grace of the Holy Spirit. An example of this is the moralistic admonition that leaders and group members are to be 'permissive' and 'accepting,' as if this were a simple human possibility, a matter of volition alone." [8]

The More of Christian Fellowship Power

This is where, I trust, the "how much more" of the healing power of Christian fellowship as compared with group dynamism depending for insight on sociological enlightenment or the motivation of humanist idealism alone deserves a hearing. This contrast between "church" and "world" has already received attention, but it could be explored much further. Since companion essays in this volume will enlarge on the ministry of interpersonal groups within church embrace, as seen from within, I limit myself to brief reminders of the "how much more" of this group power as compared with its secular rivals.

A warning, however, should precede a portrayal of this "more" or "plus." In large areas of our American church life there exists still a stubborn suspicion of human relations science (Group Dynamics). "Why, if we in the church possess the deeper insights into interpersonal relations, should our leaders subject themselves to purely secular disciplines?" Yet the very words "more" and "plus" imply the existence of a common primary base for both secular and theological insights. Both explore the problem of humanizing our common life. It is for a lack of utilizing the rich harvest of research in the dynamics of group experience even before Christian grace has had its opportunity for witness that many experiments in interpersonal fellowship in our churches have foundered.

Nevertheless, after heeding such warnings against what could be called "sanctified incompetence," the unique powers of Christian fellowship can in their turn make bold claims for attention.

A Christian fellowship, as indeed the church corporate, lays claim to the New Testament image of the Fellowship of the Holy Spirit. The church, however, has no monopoly of spirit—power as such. A teen-age gang, as was suggested earlier, can exhibit an *esprit de corps* whose dynamism for inspiring (note the root meaning of the word) a group to unified action can compare with that of a youth group within the church. The Holy Spirit which is Lord in the church has countless competitors—principalities and powers and even "spiritual hosts of wickedness in the heavenly places" (Ephesians 6:12). We of the Fellowship of the Holy Spirit are to "test these spirits" to see whether they are of God (1 John 4:1). Very well. Can any group spirit other than the Holy Spirit solve the ultimate problems of our interpersonal relations, let alone our relationship with God? Human relations science can tell us much of the gift of group acceptance and the loneliness of group rejection. But it does not presume to deal with the loneliness of guilt, of the agony of a sin-laden conscience, or the grace of divine forgiveness, or of a brotherly love which embraces enemy as well as friend.

The unique powers of the Holy Spirit in the common life of the Body of Christ could receive much further underscoring. I turn briefly, instead, to another "plus" in the ministry of interpersonal relations of which Christian fellowship is sponsor and guardian. The hundreds of groups and fellowships in our democratic society which fill meeting halls in our American towns and cities still live, so it can be claimed, on a residuum of Christian grace. Yet, in final view, do they not depend for their uniting power on some form of exclusion? Such limitation of membership may not be mere snobbery or insistence on financial or social status, as in a country club, but walls of separation are rarely if ever absent. Christian fellowships also, alas, are frequently guilty of living within enclaves of exclusion— our denominational disunity the most obvious example. Such exclusions, however, are sins against the church's own charter and foundation.

In the Body of Christ "there is neither Jew nor Greek,

neither slave nor free, neither male nor female, for you are all one in Christ Jesus" (Galatians 3:28). Here is a call to renewal of the church which interpersonal evangelism can accept with apostolic fervor. Ecumenical and interracial Christian fellowship—has this a more promising avenue for expression than in the formation of small cells of brotherliness across any and all of our exclusions? In our contacts with our fellow citizens in business or sports or political gatherings we are already latently ecumenical.

A Protestant works in office or factory side by side with a Catholic, or with a Protestant of a variant denominational loyalty. A house-church fellowship or its equivalent in our places of work or play is an incomparable opportunity for witness to our oneness—in our human solidarity first of all, and then, for all who confess loyalty to the Lord of Oneness Himself, in the Body of Christ. If Christian fellowship evangelism could rediscover its full power of witness, the atomized "lonely crowd" in our common life might see again the church fulfilling its redemptive mission in the world. It might in our time become worthy once more of the kind of amazed salute which the noted historian Adolf Harnack voiced in describing the early church:

> What a sense of stability a creation of this kind must have exercised as soon as its objects came to be understood! It was this, and not any evangelist, which proved to be the most effective missionary. In fact, we may take it as an assured fact that the mere existence and persistent activity of the individual Christian communities did more than anything else to bring about the extension of the Christian religion.[9]

4. Project Laity: Groups and Social Action

THOMAS R. BENNETT, II

Under a grant from the Philip Murray Foundation, the Department of Church and Economic Life of the National Council of Churches undertook a research project to discover how lay people were prepared by their churches for responsibility for Christian action in the world and the community. Dr. Thomas Bennett directed the study, with the results reported here. Dean of Graduate Studies at George Williams College, he is a Fellow of the National Training Laboratories, and in great demand as consultant to government, business, and volunteer agencies.

The Background of Project Laity

Much of the attention and experimentation with small groups in the local church has come from the hope that two questions could be answered: How is the participation and involvement of adults to be increased in the program of the church? Is there a way of improving the impact of the Christian laity upon the power structure and decision-making processes of the community and the world? The first of these questions has been typical in Christian adult education. The second has been central in the efforts of the churches in social action programs.

Project Laity derived both its title and its focus from the question which originated the research: What educational process needs to be developed in a local church to prepare its adult members to be "the people of God" at work in the world?

53

This question focused the twofold concern of the project. The first concern had developed from the considerable resurgence within the churches of interest "in the ministry of the laity." Within the Protestant denominations, this was focused upon the relationship of the Christian faith to the everyday problems and decisions which must be made by Christians in society. How can the Christian be prepared for his "share" in the ministry of Christ in that part of the world where each Christian must live, must work, and must somehow give evidence in his behavior of the significance of the Christian faith? Hopefully, it is within the life and program of the local church that this kind of preparation takes place. Project Laity was designed to test some specific hypotheses regarding the educational and organizational resources necessary if this expectation was to be implemented. Consequently, Project Laity was an experiment in training within the local church designed to develop both the role and the resources which would be required of clergy and members if they were to be effective in their "ministry" within the community.

A second concern in the research was with the relation of educational processes to behavioral and social change. Implicit in the program activities of the churches is the assumption that the behavior of the adult must change as a consequence of Christian commitment and church participation. A specific dimension of this change in the behavior of persons is the effort of the churches to influence the structure, processes, and relationships within the society for the promotion of social justice and human welfare. This is the traditional "social action" focus of the churches. One of the important research objectives, therefore, of Project Laity was the exploration of the nature and extent of social action in the local churches. Project Laity developed into an experiment designed to help a local church and its members become more relevantly involved in the structure, processes, and decisions of the community in which the church was located.

As an experiment, Project Laity was not developed to be an ongoing program in any local church. This meant that the

Project had a limited time both for its development and in the expectations of the persons who were involved. Second, Project Laity was designed to involve people who were not otherwise active in denominational social education and action programs. The important research question, therefore, concerned the processes by means of which a larger proportion of the potential adult participation of a local church could be engaged in social education and action programs. I was amazed to find, subsequently, that of the twenty-eight churches which participated in the Project, only one had an active social education and action group, and only three churches had the existence of such groups even indicated in their organizational structure.

One consequence of the research choice involved in the development of the Project was the introduction of a bias which excluded, by and large, persons who were knowledgeable about and active in denominational social education and action programs. Furthermore, the focus on education methodology resulted in the omission of some of the specific areas of information which we would normally associate with social action. For example, during the two-year life of the Project few of the major social issues of the time received attention in Project committees. Yet a major focus of Project committee activity had a consistent community emphasis.

I want the reader to be constantly aware that the primary issue in Project Laity was that of the *conditions influencing membership and participation in adult learning groups.* The underlying assumption was that it would be possible to isolate the forces that would be most influential in securing adult participation in a learning experience from which change in the behavior of participants and action in the community would result. If such conditions could be identified, then small groups could be developed wherein members were prepared to be active in the mission of the church in the community and in the world.

Persons, Cities, and Project Design

Project Laity was developed in three cities, each of which was located in a different section of the United States. North City was located in northern New York State. Middle City was located in northern Indiana—the main street of the Midwest. The last city was located in the mountain and plains area of the western United States and was known as West City. Twenty-eight Protestant churches representing eleven denominations were selected in the three cities to participate in the Project. There were five churches in North City; eight churches in Middle City; and, fifteen churches in West City.

The three cities were selected to ensure variation in regional characteristics and also to provide variety in population, employment, and urban growth. North City was an older manufacturing community with a population of 75,000 people. It was the center of a manufacturing and industrial area concentrated primarily in wearing apparel, electronics, and steel prefabrication. Middle City had a population of 132,000, with a heavy industrial development concentrated in electrical and electronic supplies, and light steel prefabrication. It was surrounded by an extensive rural area. West City was a large metropolitan area with over half a million in population—a major manufacturing and transportation center for the western United States. Each of the cities had an active Council of Churches which provided sponsorship for Project Laity.

The churches in Project Laity ranged from open country rural churches with a membership predominantly of nonfarm residents, to urban and suburban churches with a distribution in membership from 150 to more than 1,300 members. To the extent that was possible, churches were selected to create a reasonable cross section of Protestantism. There were three clusters of churches. The first had eight churches with a membership of 100 to 250; the second had nine churches with a membership of 350 to 500; and the third cluster consisted of eight churches with a membership from 600 to 850. In order to complete the sample there were three suburban churches with memberships of over 950 members.

There were requirements of the churches chosen for participation in the Project:

FIRST: Recognition and acceptance of the essential experimental and nonprogram function of the Project;

SECOND: Agreement to continue participation in the Project for the duration of the experiment. Although this did not preclude withdrawal, it did provide a means for securing data should any group decide to withdraw;

THIRD: Development of a Project committee from each church of at least eight but no more than fifteen members, one-half of the membership coming from persons who were not involved in leadership positions but were active participating members in the congregation; and,

FOURTH: Guarantee of the participation of both the clergy and the members of a Project committee in the training process which was used to initiate Project Laity within each of the cities.

A series of interviews with members of Project committees and the clergy of participating churches was used to develop a regular reporting process for all the Project committee meetings. Each Project committee supplied a report on the content of the discussion of each meeting, a group observation process on member participation, and individual post-meeting reaction questionnaires which were completed by each person attending any meeting of the committee. In addition, I personally interviewed each Project committee every sixty to ninety days in order to obtain additional information on what was happening in the groups.

It is unnecessary for the purposes of this chapter to provide an extensive review of the design of Project Laity. Through interviews and questionnaires detailed information was obtained on each of the participating clergy, on the congregations of the churches in Project Laity, and on the membership of the Project committees. The project officially continued for twenty months. A training "clinic" was held for both the clergy and lay members of the Project committees. The laity met for five evenings during one week in sessions of two to three hours per evening. The clergy met for five mornings during that week for sessions that lasted from three to four hours.

The focus of the training for the laity was upon the development of group membership skills. Each evening session was in two parts: the first was a demonstration or practice experience in which everyone participated and which identified a functional need within a learning group. A brief lecture then followed the demonstration experience, presenting the relevant information which would further elaborate what participants had already identified and experienced. It was important that each Project committee receive training in the following:

> The characteristics of group goals and their relation to the attractiveness and productivity of a Project committee.
>
> The effect of member acceptance and rejection upon the way in which people communicated within the group and upon the group problem-solving procedures.
>
> The necessary membership functions related to accomplishing group tasks and to building the interpersonal relationships which would be necessary for group effectiveness.
>
> The steps involved in program planning and goal formation.

The rationale for this training experience was that it would increase the sensitivity of committee members to one another and to the processes and problems of their own group development.

The training experience for the clergy was similar to that of the laity, but there were two major differences. First, the clergy were given an experience in sensitivity training designed to provide self-insight about their own behavior and leadership in groups. A major purpose of this sensitivity training was to help the clergy develop some flexibility in their characteristic ways of relating to church members and of functioning in the groups in which they found themselves. Second, a greater emphasis upon problem-solving processes and skills was provided in the training for the clergy. This was based on the assumption that they were persons of special competence who could provide important assistance in group problem-solving and decision-making situations.

This special training for the clergy was based upon a specific hypothesis that the continuity and effectiveness of a committee would be dependent upon the flexibility of the clergy in being able to surrender traditional roles and status in their relationship to members. As a consequence of this hypothesis, the clergy were asked to exclude themselves deliberately from any designated leadership position within a developing Project committee. The ministers were to function as members of the committee, but not in their designated leadership position in the church. This request was designed to provide me with data on the role ambiguity and conflict which ministers would experience, and at the same time to study the processes which would emerge by which each Project committee would resolve the group leadership issue.

The final session of each training clinic was a joint meeting of the ministers with the members of the Project committee from their church. During this final meeting the resource leaders who had been involved in each of the clinics assisted each Project committee to identify the significant learning which had occurred in the experience for each member, and to develop plans for the immediate future meetings of a committee. This was the first full meeting of each of the Project committees, and following this concluding session of the training experience, most of the committees met within the following month. Project Laity had begun.

What Happened in the Project Committees?

I had anticipated that the initial stage of development of the Project committees would be similar among the committees, regardless of their location and composition, and would be shaped primarily by the impact of the training experience. A preoccupation with the training experience and its consequences for members was precisely what emerged in the early sessions of Project committees. What was particularly significant, however, was the increase of interpersonal sensitivity among members and the extent of appreciation and concern which members generally shared for one another. Members found that the committees were more personally important to them than any they had usually experienced in church groups, or in other organizations in which they regularly participated. Most of the committees spent from two to five meetings reliving the training experience, sharing its personal consequences, and slowly beginning to confront the unresolved issues of goals and leadership needs. During some of my first interviews with Project committees, I pointed out that part of the fascination with the training experience was in the avoidance of having to develop meaningful tasks and confront the leadership struggles which had emerged in many of the groups.

The tension created within Project committees by the absence of designated content to be "learned" during their meetings and specifically formulated goals externally imposed, produced initial efforts to formulate direction quite early in the life of every group. The most typical evidence of this effort was the attention given to the development of "projects." Suggestions for such projects began to appear between the third and seventh meetings, with the majority of the groups attempting to make some selection upon which to work. The important point is that all the project suggestions originated from the members of a group; they did not come from program resources, my suggestion, or any other explicit direction provided by the Project. These projects were, therefore, the means by which the committees worked out the problems of learning content and goals, and at the same time the project proposals were a source for member satisfaction and group productivity.

Three types of projects were developed. The first and most common was the attempt to create, either for a specific group within the church or for the designated leadership of the churches' program, a training experience similar to that which Project committees had experienced. Where there were persons or groups in the community which could provide the training assistance necessary or where denominational personnel could be helpful, most of these training projects were carried through by committees.

A second type of project focused on the relationship of the Christian faith to the daily work of participants. Many committees designed and undertook extensive study and discussion programs—some lasting nearly a year—where primary attention was given to providing individual members the opportunity to explore and discuss the ethical dilemmas which they did experience as Christians in their occupations. When one recognizes that one-third of the committees were meeting at least twice a month, then it is readily understood that such personally focused discussions developed an intense group life among the committees.

I had not expected that this type of project would disclose the central issue that was to determine whether a committee continued to the completion of Project Laity or terminated at an earlier time. This central issue was a focal conflict experienced by all the committees—the establishment of a level of interpersonal intimacy within the group which provided sufficient trust that members could explore distinctively personal issues, the majority of which were related to occupational and professional crisis situations. In one way or another, each of the committees experienced this focal conflict, and its resolution determined the survival of that committee.

A third type of project was directly related to operational problems in the existing program of the church. Frequently the problems selected for committee activity were crisis situations which had already received attention and work by other committees or groups within the church, but where this prior effort had resulted in factions that only further polarized the problem and intensified the underlying conflict. For example, one Project committee worked for most of its life on overcoming a conflict situation within the congregation that had resulted from an extended fight between the church leadership and a former pastor. Another committee became the fact-finding and mediating group within a church that was experiencing severe conflict over a decision about relocation. All the committees which undertook projects of this type had one common characteristic. *They focused upon operational problems in the church because there did not exist within the church structure any committee or group which could undertake experimentation,* with its obvious risks in the resolution of the operational difficulties or conflict situations.

This means that when confronted with a conflict, the existing committees and groups of the local church were already so committed to predetermined goals and program strategies that they were inflexible and incapable of response to the crisis. Project committees, in contrast, had no imposed goals, no predetermined program content, and no fixed leadership structure. But they did have training in problem-solving, in leadership skills, and in the processes of group development. They were, therefore, a natural arena for the exploration and resolution of intergroup conflict within the church.

No one should suppose that all of the twenty-eight churches that began in Project Laity were still active at its conclusion. I developed a classification to describe what happened to committees in terms of whether or not they continued participation throughout the Project. There were twelve *Continuing Committees,* which maintained operation from the beginning of the Project to its termination, and five of these committees were still active three years after the conclusion of Project Laity. There were seven *Terminating Committees,* which continued their activity beyond the first two months of the Project but ceased working at some point prior to the terminal date. Then there were seven *Abortive Committees,* none of which survived the first two months of Project Laity. Of this group, five withdrew from the Project at the request of their ministers. In my interviews with the ministers involved, it was clear to me that the ambiguity and the permissiveness required in Project Laity had been experienced as too threatening to the usual patterns of control and direction that these ministers had used. The withdrawal of the Abortive Committees was almost entirely due to decision and action by the minister; the Terminating Committees ceased their work as a consequence of a crisis in relationships experienced by all the members of the group. The Continuing Committees were able to function as cohesive, problem-solving groups involving their total membership, *including the ministers.* Consequently, the most important results obtained from Project Laity were those which helped to identify what made it possible for some committees to continue and made it necessary for others to terminate.

It would be easy to explain the difference by assuming that it must be in the composition of the groups. I attempted the same explanation, but the extensive statistical information I had on the groups quickly destroyed my effort. The membership of Continuing Committees did tend to be slightly older, to have the highest income, and to have slightly more persons who were professionally employed. None of these characteristics, however, nor differences in education, length of residence in the community, and church membership were statistically important. The only, and most important, difference between the two groups was that the members of Continuing Committees reported the highest involvement in other community organizations. Nearly half the members of these groups were involved in three or more community organizations. I could not ignore the fact that the busiest people in the community were also the ones who found time for the intensive involvement required in Project Laity, *although half of them were not involved in the leadership of their church.* Since that time I have not been impressed by ministerial complaints about "the way members work for other organizations but not their church." The unpleasant truth may be that what the church provides as an invitation to involvement is not worth the required work.

Some Significant Results from the Research

1. *Group process training is essential for the development of effective small groups.* It is certainly possible to assemble a group of people and trust to the fortunes of interaction to develop the necessary relationships for member productivity

and satisfaction. It is precisely this haphazard approach to group design and development which accounts for the high mortality rate in the group-centered program of churches. Although Project Laity experienced a high loss rate, both Continuing and Terminating Committees maintained levels of group activity for lengths of time which exceeded other small group experiments.

The division of Project groups into Continuing and Terminating Committees in no way reflects a negative impact of the training experience upon members. The only deviation between the two was that the Terminating Committees reported a much higher response to the *increased interpersonal sensitivity* of members, whereas among the members of Continuing Committees the higher response was in the *improvement of group skills* among members. My explanation for this is that, in relation to the frustrations experienced in the later history of their groups, the members of a Terminating Committee were able to look back upon the training experience as a moment that was most productive in personal learning and "successful" in their group life. With the Continuing Committees, however, the later activity of their groups placed the training experience as simply the initial stage of their group development, and encouraged them to examine the impact of that experience upon the total effectiveness of their committee performance.

There is no question that the training experience did result in increased interpersonal sensitivity for persons participating in Project Laity. There is equally no question but that the training experience facilitated the development of the relevant membership and leadership skills which helped the committees in both their problem-solving and their maintenance of the group. The essential difference was that in Continuing Committees group standards and procedures emerged which reinforced their use of the training experience. It is my belief that part of this utilization must be related to the higher percentage of members in Continuing Committees who had extensive nonchurch group experience and involvement.

2. *The greater a group's permissiveness toward individual goal achievement, the more the person will attempt change and express satisfaction with the group.* One of the central functions of the training experience was to help committee members develop the appropriate group functions and skills which would enable them to supply effective support to one another. At the same time, however, it must not be forgotten that Project Laity was designed to provide a condition of *maximum permissiveness* within each group. There was no imposed learning goal, no designated content for the meetings, nor was there any designated leadership. This created a vacuum which had to be filled by the contributions and leadership of group members. At the same time, this increased the anxiety of persons in the committees, especially during the earlier sessions. While this occurred, it also provided the setting in which members had an increased opportunity to identify their own personal learning objectives and needs. The maximum permissiveness of the committees enabled their members to identify specific changes in their own behavior with which they wished to experiment and also to focus on the conditions within the group which were necessary to encourage and support this individual effort.

The experience of Continuing Committees is decisive on this point. Members in these groups experienced the highest degree of satisfaction with both the personal consequences of their participation and with the conditions which they experienced within the committee. These committees consistently reported that their highest satisfaction came from the opportunity for self-expression and the freedom of communication with the group, and especially as these conditions were related to the acceptance which persons experienced in their own efforts to pursue learning goals that were personally important. The consistent theme was that the major satisfaction was with personal growth, which had been facilitated by the freedom and flexibility experienced within the committee. The open communication and the intimacy among members was characterized as the major support for this satisfaction. Within the

Terminating Committees, in contrast, the content and goals tended to be more rigidly defined, rather than being allocated to a designated leadership structure to supply procedural direction. The Terminating Committees were characterized by a greater rigidity in their structure and by a significantly reduced level of intimacy and flexibility.

3. *The development of trust emerges from the confrontation of conflict.* The primary contrast between Continuing and Terminating Committees was in the level of intimacy among members. The establishment of this level became a focal conflict in every committee. Such a focal conflict emerged whenever a situation became so tense that it displaced group efforts toward its resolution, before a committee had sufficient energy to proceed to the definition of its learning goals and content. Generally speaking, the focal conflicts experienced by the committees were either in the relationship of member needs to committee goals, or were occasioned by the issue of the level of intimacy necessary to establish sufficient trust among members so that the committee could function as a total group. The Continuing Committees were able to carry through an explicit confrontation of their conflict around acceptance and trust. The result was the establishment of appropriate group standards both for the management of conflict and for defining what trust really meant for persons in the group. This became as elemental and open as persons frankly discussing with one another the extent to which they were able to accept each other and to confront together the issues around which they experienced both trust and distrust of one another.

4. *The development of trust and intimacy in the groups was increased to the degree that there was a significant change in the behavior of the clergy.* Project Laity was designed so that it required increased role flexibility on the part of the ministers involved. By stipulating that they could not function in positions of designated leadership, the performance of their more traditionally authority-oriented roles was inhibited. The ministers were required to change from their usual position of designated leader in a group to developing behavior appropri-

ate for functioning as a resource person. This meant that they had to function as group members who possessed a specialized competency and skills which could assist the committee in its problem-solving efforts, but which could not be used for directing the group.

I had predicted that the ministers would experience two types of conflict in their committee participation. The first of these would be role conflict within the committee, due to the inhibiting of their traditional authority-oriented roles. A second conflict would occur around their capacity to trust the group sufficiently to share with the members the stress which the minister was experiencing in his attempted role change. Again the Continuing Committees supply the crucial data. All the clergy participating in these groups reported that they acquired increased sensitivity to others and significantly changed their behavior. Furthermore, they were able to share with the groups the conflicts which they experienced and to identify the changes which they were attempting in their behavior. This in turn was openly supported by committee members. In short, the effort of the minister to change his behavior became a support for the development of trust in the committee, and this again became a reinforcement for the behavior change attempted by the minister. All the Continuing Committees reported significant changes in the behavior of their ministers; with one exception, members of Terminating Committees reported minimum change in the behavior of their clergy. I think the implication of this result is self-evident for any minister who wishes to encourage the development of small groups within the church.

5. *Availability of external resources and skilled consultant help is essential for the development of effective small groups in the local church.* In the design of Project Laity, all the churches in West City were related, through an associate project director, to adult education agencies and denominational agencies programming groups that were resident in the area. In contrast, the project churches in Middle and North City were dependent upon the infrequent, but periodic visits

which I was able to make for any additional assistance. In West City there was only a 30 per cent loss in the total number of committees participating, while in Middle and North City the losses were 70 and 90 per cent respectively. The critical issue was whether or not consultant help increased the vital potential of these small groups.

In the case of North City and Middle City, the design of Project Laity most nearly duplicated the characteristic pattern of programming services of denominational agencies, namely, the diffusion of program materials, guides, and other printed resources accompanied by occasional visits of specialized personnel. In the case of West City, the committees were related to the total range of available training and information resources that existed in the community. The consequence of this was that the committees in the West City reported that consultant help was available when needed and was directly related to their improved committee effectiveness. In contrast, the committees in the other two cities were consistent in reporting that consultant help was needed but was not available at the critical points in their history.

Some Implications for Future Reference

Within the experience that I have reported, one point is especially clear. It is difficult in today's world for a Christian to confront the dilemmas of daily living. It is even more difficult to make responsible Christian choices if there is no place within the local church for an intimate sharing of the burdens, the joys, and the consequences of Christian behavior. Worship can provide that moment of sharing and personal confrontation in the presence of God, but what the Christian needs most is the face-to-face support and criticism of his fellow Christians. This is best provided in small groups developed for this purpose.

Yet the program of most local churches is not designed, at least at present, and except in rare instances, to provide this kind of small group opportunity in which the ethical dilemmas of daily Christian living can be exposed and analyzed, and a more vigorous Christian witness formulated. Whatever else may have happened in Project Laity, this was the kind of experience which members had month after month in their committee sessions. I lived these experiences with them in interviews and in committee meetings. This was one moment within the life of the church and within their own personal vicissitudes where members could be assured of a group of persons willing to listen, support, criticize, and above all, encourage the Christian life.

The experience of the committees discloses the difficulty of achieving a sufficient level of intimacy and trust in small face-to-face groups to enable persons to share with any depth the Christian concerns which they actually have. The realistic difficulty of this kind of human encounter is too frequently glossed over in the church by intellectualized discussions of the meaning of "love." The issue of trust alone became the breaking-point for all the committees. Continuing and Terminating Committees emerged as a result of their confrontation of this issue.

A continued existence, even for research purposes, became possible for those groups able explicitly to confront the need for a level of intimacy and trust that would permit the most personal sharing of experience beneficial to all members. For those committees in which it was not possible explicitly to confront the issues of intimacy and trust, and for which the problem became primarily one of orderly procedure and structure in leadership, the issue of trust was resolved by terminating the group. These were groups unable, in the final analysis, to supply the full extent and depth of the experience which members needed with one another.

There was no lack of prayer in these groups. There was no lack of loving motivation. There was no evidence of a lack of commitment to try to succeed. *What were absent were the relevant skills, and in most cases, the explicit identifiable support of the ministers.* The underlying issue, therefore, remains; if daily Christian living is to have depth, then its dilemmas must be exposed. To expose these personal dilemmas requires a level of trust and intimacy in our relationships with others which appears difficult to attain in most church groups. Yet that difficulty can be overcome by relevant training experiences and by a willingness on the part of ministers to explore and expose the conflicts of their own humanness.

The most imperative, and at the same time most difficult, form of social action for a local church is that which may be required to exert significant Christian influence upon the affairs of its own community. Whether the issues are social, economic, inter-group, and the political problems of the nation and the world; or whether they are the immediate problems of a deteriorating neighborhood, increasing deliquency rates, racial conflict, or corrupt practices in local government, the problem for the individual Christian is essentially the same. Unless the Christian is already interested and involved in such social issues (and few persons are in the churches) then the essential problem is one of developing a base of operation within the church. The best base is to be found in a small group of persons who are willing to be involved in such issues, and without this group support it is difficult, if not impossible, for the individual Christian to conceive of himself as potentially effective against social problems. He is in an inadequate and exposed position to control the personal threat and anxiety which such issues will arouse. Exhortation and persuasion are not functional responses; an effective small group is more useful.

This was seen within Project committees which, within their own communities, took upon themselves in a publicly responsible way some of the most controversial issues confronting their community life. I found committees becoming information centers, initiators of effective action, and, in a number of instances, champions of unpopular community causes. Yet initially not one single member conceived of Project Laity as a social action project. Social action came as an inevitable expression of Christian confrontation with an environment which required some type of corrective response. Social action was the consequence of a compelling Christian faith; it was not a "program."

My experience in Project Laity has made it clear that the conditions within the local church have a priority of influence upon its goals and programs which cannot be underestimated. If there are identifiable conflicts within the structure or the program of the local church, any plan or change effort within that church will reflect a preoccupation with such conflict. This is understandable in view of the fact that the members of a local church are primarily concerned with the survival of the congregation with which they are personally identified.

Local church conflicts or tension situations must be resolved before goals and programs designed by denominational agencies will be accepted and implemented. In those areas of local church life where denominational goals and activities are perceived to threaten the existence of the current program and commitment of the congregation, the denominational organization will be correspondingly resisted. What this suggests is that goals, programs, and change efforts which are primarily determined and designed for the local congregation by denominational agencies form perhaps the most ineffective approach to planned changes within that congregation.

The final implication which I must emphasize is the importance of the behavior of the clergy for facilitating change in the values and actions of church members. The crucial issue which confronts the minister is not what to say, but rather what kind of a person to be. Within the Project committees the behavior of the ministers was a focal point in the changes which members were seeking for themselves. Where the clergy demonstrated an increased sensitivity to the needs of other members, shared explicitly their feelings about the process being developed, and attained a degree of role flexibility, they gave effective and appropriate leadership in the problem-solving activities of committees and in the personal changes being attempted by members.

Unfortunately, many ministers have developed stereotypic behavior based on traditional role models of the clergy as preacher and teacher, without developing a sensitivity to the situational needs of the local church and the real-life issues of persons. The most frequent tendency of the minister is to focus his attention upon the goals of the church and to try to develop an appropriate plan for their attainment without paying adequate attention to the role he must perform in the various interpersonal and group situations in which he must function. The most important contribution of Project Laity to the ministers who participated in it was that it increased their capacity to diagnose what they needed to do in the various group situations in which they found themselves.

The local church can be a source of preparation and support to enable the laity to be the people of God at work in the world. There are few traditional models for a ministry which can be utilized; what is required is an intensive and extensive problem-solving process in which church members thoroughly participate. Denominational programming units will confront the need for radical redesigning to assist in the development of more adequate, person-oriented educational processes in the local church. At the same time, the result of the training experience used to initiate Project Laity demonstrates that both resources and willingness can be created within the local church, in order to bring about those changes in persons and community which Christians must and can develop if their life in the world is to make its impact.

5. Elements of Group Behavior

EUGENE E. LAUBACH

Although the behavior of any particular group has elements of unpredictability, the basic patterns of its life are now well mapped and understood. Dr. Laubach describes some of these basic factors in this chapter. His broad experience as minister of Methodist churches, and as Minister of Education and now as Executive Minister of the Riverside Church in New York, and Lecturer in the Department of Religion and Psychiatry at Union Theological Seminary, qualify him to deal with this subject in both its theoretical and its practical aspects.

Any person seeking to work in a group setting, or involved in helping a group reach its full potential, needs to have some basic tools for diagnosing what is going on in a group. Although the persons in each group provide a constellation of factors which make it unique, there are some elements of group life which are consistently present in all groups. A knowledge of these enables both group leaders and group members to work more effectively. The purpose of this chapter is to help describe some of the behaviors, some form of which will be present in all group settings. Obviously there are innumerable possibilities for description. The choice here has been limited to a few basic concepts without which a leader cannot operate effectively.

Perhaps at the beginning a word needs to be said about that misused term "group dynamics." Unfortunately, in the minds of some people this piece of jargon has come to mean a special set of techniques used "on" a group for purposes of control

73

or manipulation. In actual fact, persons were interacting in groups long before their behavior was described in any scientific manner. A group cannot choose to have or not to have group dynamics. It always has some kind of dynamics going in its activity. What it can choose is whether it will improve its way of functioning by trying to understand its own dynamics. The group behaviorists have helped us understand that as we can make visible the patterns by which groups function, we can help groups operate in increasingly effective ways both at the level of productivity and the level of personal satisfaction.

The term "group dynamics" was used to identify the theoretical structure for describing the structures of social groups developed by Kurt Lewin, a German emigrant with a basic orientation in Gestalt psychology. He saw groups in terms of a "field theory" which included both the forces in a group which made for group unity and cohesiveness and the forces which assisted or frustrated the group in moving toward a goal. These two dimensions introduce the first of the technical terms which are part of the language of groups.

Some Dimensions of Group Interaction

Group interactions have a variety of dimensions. The following are some of the more visible ones:

1. *Task*

One of the primary characteristics of a group is that it is always engaged in doing something. Its members are involved in a *task*. The task at hand may be to plan a program, to select a staff member, to become informed on a specific topic, to organize, to achieve a long-range goal. Any of these are tasks which may be the focus of a group at a given time. Sometimes the tasks are quite explicit. They may be listed formally in an agenda. At other times a group may be working on a task which it does not even recognize. Sometimes various members of the group are working at odds because they do not share a common perception of what the task really is.

The classic example is the task-oriented behavior of a teacher who insists on teaching his prepared lesson no matter how inappropriate it may be to the real needs of the group, or the group leader who hurries through a whole agenda rather than consulting with group members about which items could be more fruitfully postponed.

2. *Maintenance*

At the same time that members of a group are engaged in a task, they are also engaged in another activity, that of maintaining themselves as persons in the context of this group. This means simply that they want, because of their participation in this group, to feel enhanced as individuals, aware of their own worth and supported by their relations in this group. This dimension is the "feeling" level of their group experience and has to do with their sense that this group is an important group to belong to and that it is one where they experience personal satisfaction.

3. *The Problem of Imbalance*

Part of the difficulty groups get into is that one or the other of these two elements becomes too strong. If the task behavior of the group members dominates too greatly, members of the group may feel pressured, railroaded, unable to make themselves heard or understood. Pressure mounts and decisions get made before proposed solutions have been adequately tested. Group members begin to feel uncomfortable and threatened, although they may not understand why.

The situation is equally unsatisfactory when the group is overweighed on behavior calculated to maintain its members. There are some groups that literally cannot make decisions because they fear that some members will "have their feelings hurt." When much of a group's energy has to be devoted toward making the members "feel good," there is less energy available to achieve meaningful tasks. Their productivity and decision-making ability are seriously handicapped.

4. *Need for Both Dimensions*

There are two important implications for persons who work with groups. The first is the importance of achieving a balance of these two kinds of behavior, so that the group can 1) achieve tasks and 2) feel good about its work. Part of the needed skill for any group leader (or any informed group participant) is the sensitivity to diagnose what is going on at a given time and to act in such a way as to supply some of the kinds of behavior that the group lacks. If a leader perceives that his group is under pressure to achieve a task, and task achievement behavior dominates, he can engage in behavior which supports group members. He may be sure persons know each other, may help persons gain the floor to speak. He may acknowledge that he is interested in what persons are saying by listening intently and receiving contributions. If maintenance-centered behavior is too dominant the leader may help balance the group by engaging in behavior which encourages moving toward achievement of the task. He may help the group define its purpose, ask for information or give it, elicit opinions from group members, clarify ambiguous areas, etc. His aim is to help provide the balance which makes for maximum group functioning.

5. *We Tend to Repeat One Pattern*

Research has shown that almost all persons are more comfortable in one set of these behaviors than with another. We tend to operate more naturally and consistently either at task or maintenance behavior. There are almost no persons who are equally competent. But persons who lead groups can expand their competencies by practice and experimentation. The leader or group member most useful to the group is the person who can sense which style of behavior is most needed and act to provide it. To do this takes a careful awareness of one's own behavior as well as skill in accurately perceiving what is really going on in the group over a given period of time.

Some of the key behaviors have been classified and are listed below. Every leader should examine his own characteristic patterns, asking himself "What do I do most often? How do I see myself?" It is helpful to check perceptions with others who see us in group settings and to see whether we see ourselves as others see us. Once a leader knows his own most frequent pattern, he can begin to experiment deliberately with new roles of behavior to expand the range of his own usefulness to a group. Some of the more easily identifiable clusters of behavior which apply equally to group members and group leaders are:

Task Functions

1. *Initiator:* Proposing tasks or goals; defining a group problem; suggesting a procedure or ideas for solving a problem . . .
2. *Information-seeker:* Requesting facts; seeking relevant information about a group concern . . .
3. *Information-giver:* Offering facts; providing relevant information about a group concern . . .
4. *Opinion-seeker:* Asking for expressions of feeling; requesting a statement of estimate; soliciting expressions of value; seeking suggestions and ideas . . .
5. *Opinion-giver:* Stating a belief about a matter before the group; giving suggestions and ideas . . .
6. *Clarifier:* Interpreting ideas or suggestions; clearing up confusions; defining terms; indicating alternatives and issues before the group . . .
7. *Elaborator:* Giving examples; developing meanings; making generalizations; indicating how a proposal might work out, if adopted . . .
8. *Summarizer:* Pulling together related ideas; restating suggestions after the group has discussed them; offering a decision or conclusion for the group to accept or reject . . .

Maintenance Functions

1. *Encourager:* Being friendly, warm, and responsive to others; accepting others and their contributions; regarding others by giving them an opportunity or recognition . . .
2. *Sensitizer:* Expressing the feeling of the group; calling attention to reactions of the group to ideas and suggestions; sharing his own feeling or affect with other members . . .
3. *Harmonizer:* Attempting to reconcile disagreements; reducing

tension through "pouring oil on troubled waters"; getting people to explore their differences . . .

4. *Compromiser:* When his own ideas or status are involved in a conflict, offering compromise yielding status, admitting error, disciplining himself to maintain group cohesion . . .

5. *Gate-keeper:* Attempting to keep communication channels open; facilitating the participation of others; suggesting procedures for sharing opportunity to discuss group problems . . .

6. *Standard-setter:* Expressing standards for the group to achieve; applying standards in evaluating group functioning and production . . .

7. *Process-observer:* Observation of various aspects of group process and feedback of such data with proposed interpretations into the group's evaluation of its own procedures . . .

8. *Supporter:* Going along with movement of the group; accepting ideas of others; serving as an interested audience . . .

In trying to gain perspective on our own behavior in groups it is important to see patterns rather than single acts. Interestingly enough, people seem quite visible to others in a group, and there is a good deal of agreement about who does what kind of thing with frequency.

Group Conflict

As groups of persons work together they inevitably experience times when the individual freedoms of group members must be limited in order to achieve group goals. Members of a group do not share common goals at the beginning of their time together, and personal differences make it almost impossible for them to share a common frame of reference. The inevitable result is that there are differences of opinion, differences of perception, and experiences of conflict within the group. Conflict itself is not negative. It is how it is handled that gives it its positive or negative values. How a group handles its conflict tells a great deal about its level of maturity. Research has shown that groups react in some patterns which are quite characteristic.

1. *Flight Reactions*

One response to conflict is to run from it, to exhibit behavior which moves them away from the conflict itself or to "take flight." This form of behavior may take many forms. The topic may be suddenly changed, a personal incident may divert group interest, a joke may shift a mood, an announcement of refreshments may foreclose further discussion. On some occasions, this may be extremely helpful to a group. To get out from under stress for a while may give them the chance to regroup and rebuild so that they can come back later and deal more effectively with the situation. However, flight may be an inappropriate pattern in circumstances where a group needs to work through rather than evade conflict. Flight is inappropriate when it is the *only* reaction of individuals or groups to conflict.

2. *Fight Reactions*

Another characteristic response to conflict is "fight." Fight may be "intragroup"—centered on some matter that threatens to divide the group; or "extragroup"—an attack on an issue, or individuals, or other groups outside the fighting group itself. Some persons as well as some groups are highly adapted to this response. As a response it is neither positive nor negative in itself. Its value depends on the circumstances. There are times when a difference of opinion is pronounced enough and the conflict of interest sharp enough that the only way to deal with it is to fight it out. Any married couple will testify that there are times when a good fight will clear the air and enable reconciliation to take place. At times in groups, this is the most productive response to conflict. Fight can be a negative response, however, when it splits the group farther and farther apart so that reconciliation becomes less and less possible. Some "fight reactions" may be a form of flight which divert a group from its purpose.

3. *Dependency Reactions*

A third kind of response to conflict is "dependency." Dependency occurs in situations where conflict is *not* an element, but it is promoted when conflict does arise. Faced with a conflict of interests or opinion the group seeks an outside authority to come and settle their problems for them. This is one of the worst snares for the group leader, for it is so ego-building to a leader to be needed and wanted. But the leader who succumbs finds that it is a trap from which there is no escape. By allowing the group to become dependent upon him, he has limited the development of their own resources. He has also bound himself to carry the burden of their dependency on himself. The leader weighs carefully requests by the group to "tell them what to do." The only time he can legitimately accede without serious consequences is when he possesses special information or resources which only he can supply. More often, he needs to reject attempts by the group to become dependent upon him because he realizes he cannot fulfill this role or live up to such a responsibility. If a group is to become mature and productive, its members must learn, no matter how painfully, to assume responsibility for the group. No leader has the right to deny them that opportunity. Many church groups have fallen into serious dependency problems with their pastors which gravely inhibit their use of their own resources to solve their problems.

4. *Counterdependency*

Another group phenomenon in relation to conflict and leadership can be described by the term "counterdependency." It is the opposite side of the dependent reactions described. In most dependent reactions there is a counterdependent reaction as well. In dependency, group members say "Tell us what to do." Counterdependent behavior says "You can't tell me anything." The child who goes to Sunday School because his parents say so may be dependent. The adolescent who refuses to do so *because* his parents say so is exhibiting counterdependent behavior. The difficulty with this kind of behavior is that it takes its cues from others and it reacts *against,* rather than from any positive convictions. Thus it may block out helpful resources and sound advice.

Counterdependence lends itself to manipulation as much as dependency. The group leader who feels the rejection of his role from counterdependent group members needs to know that it may be a role rejection rather than a personal one, and that it may have nothing to do with the effectiveness of his leadership. His insight into what is happening can keep him from needless personal anxiety about himself or his performance.

5. *Interdependence*

Uncritical dependence or counterdependence keeps persons and groups at the child and adolescent level rather than helping them become mature adults capable of making decisions of their own. Genuine independence comes when individuals, or groups, recognize that there are some occasions when leaders, or authorities, may be right and some when they need to be challenged. True independence is achieved when members of a group accept responsibility for making their own decisions and carrying them out. In doing so, each member understands his responsibility for contributing his particular resources to the group and acknowledges the particular ways in which he needs the group to help him.

6. *Our Reactions Vary*

In situations of conflict groups may exhibit behavior which could be described by one or perhaps all of the above categories. It is important to note that in every group there are some persons who thrive on conflict and others who are greatly bothered by it. A group leader needs some awareness of his own attitudes toward the presence of conflict and his own characteristic patterns of dealing with it. As in the task-maintenance area, such self-awareness comes from practice and experience, and from honest "feedback" from other persons who have an opportunity to observe us in action.

7. Conflict is Not Necessarily Negative

As we have already seen, conflict can be positive as well as negative in its outcome. Yet there persists an assumption in many church groups that conflict is bad. No matter how much we are in opposition, says this point of view, we should not allow it to become visible. Such an attitude frequently sends conflict underground, with the result that it appears in inappropriate places where the real issues cannot be dealt with. A mature group recognizes that it must make conflict a legitimate part of its life together and use it as a constructive force. Conflict may serve a useful purpose in a group when it reveals deep commitments to points of view which are held by group members. By identifying the areas of conflict, a group may recognize its need to find a solution which contains key elements of both points of view. By accepting the legitimacy of more than one position, the group makes possible honest and responsible conflict which may lead to more constructive solutions.

Conflict can become positive when group members are personally secure enough that they may dare to be open and honest with each other. In other words, the more group members have a sense of being maintained, the more they trust each other, the more they dare recognize and tolerate conflict and difference. The amount of conflict a group can handle without being fractured reveals how mature a group has become.

Leadership in Problem-Solving

One of the most widespread myths about the field of group dynamics is that the less the leader does, the more democratic he is. This is a distortion of a central truth about leadership. Research has shown that autocratic leadership over an extended period will tend to make a group more dependent upon that central authority and less trustful of its own resources. It may also breed a latent counterdependence which may express itself in thinly disguised acts of hostility. On the other hand, completely *laissez-faire* leadership which draws no guidelines tends to promote anxiety and disequilibrium in the group. One of the chief insights about leadership is that successful leaders are those who are able to shift their leadership performance to help meet group needs. Since needs change as a group matures, these leaders need also to be adaptable in the form of help they provide.

This can be most clearly illustrated in the process of group problem-solving.

Problem-solving is one of the continuous processes of life. At every point in life all persons are presented with choices to be made, questions to be resolved, problems which must be answered.

The levels at which persons go about solving their problems vary:

1. *Logical-Rational*

At first thought, problem-solving seems simple. There are logical, rational processes by which we can reach conclusions. At this level problem-solving is seen as an abstract process in which problems are defined, information gathered, alternatives tested and solutions reached. We sometimes feel that solutions ought not to be affected by other factors such as personal feelings and group forces. Unfortunately, few individuals or groups can operate only at the rational level. They must therefore deal with two other dimensions as well.

2. *Personal Feelings*

Each person carries in himself a whole range of feelings, assumptions, expectations, needs, skills, and information. They help determine what is or is not a problem for him and what will be the range of his choices of possible solutions.

3. *Group Forces*

In addition to these individual forces there are some forces being exerted in group interaction, such as whether assumptions are shared, perceptions of whether the group has competence to perform its task, and how the group will manage the conflict which differences of opinion will generate.

Few group members or leaders fully understand that groups are operating at all three levels—the logical, the level of personal needs, the level of group interaction. To meet all these needs simultaneously, a leader must be highly aware of a process through which a group must move in solving its problems. Only if the leader can understand which phase of the process the group is engaged in can he be helpful with appropriate behavior.

4. *The Process of Problem-Solving in Groups*

An analysis of the process through which a group moves might look something like this:

A. *Defining the problem.* At this phase the group needs help in clarifying the nature of the problem that is at issue and its implications for the group. There needs to be common agreement among the group members about what is actually the central problem and what are the subsidiary concerns. Leadership behavior to help the group along could come either from the stated leader or any group member. A procedural help would be the possibility of using a buzz group to get at quick definition of the problem. The leader will want to watch out for the tendency to be too general and vague, or the tendency to rush into solving the problem before it is stated. As he blocks such attempts he aids the group in achieving its task. An important part of this step is the enlistment of personal feelings about the problem as entering into the definition. Not only what we *think* about the problem, but what we *feel* must be caught up in the definition we give it.

B. *Developing possible solutions.* After the problem is defined, the group needs to create as many alternative solutions to it as possible. The process most conducive to this is called "stockpiling" and means simply compiling possibilities without evaluating them. This is a critical phase in group problem-solving, and one most frequently violated. The leader must be alert to avoid moving into an evaluation weighing and sifting process until many ideas have been brought forward. He must encourage expression of ideas, even those which seem unlikely as ultimate solutions. The group which cuts off this process will shortchange itself in the amount of material it has to work with.

C. *Sifting, weighing, and evaluating solutions.* At this phase the stockpile of solutions is evaluated by the group and reduced to some manageable alternatives. The leader may help a group do this by assisting them in clarifying, testing the validity or reality of some proposals, evaluating implications. He will help avoid the danger of having proposals "labeled" by being connected too closely with the persons who suggested them. One method is to list all proposals and establish that they have now become group property, not "John's idea." Again, the leader must be alert for group behavior which moves toward prematurely deciding on one proposal before all have been examined. He helps the group with procedures of testing points where there is agreement and in ultimately voting on the one proposal that the group will implement.

D. *Converting decision to action.* In this phase many groups, pleased with having made a decision, fail to pin down how the decision will be implemented and who is to be responsible for carrying it out. Sometimes a large group will attempt to work out trivial details which should have been given to a committee. Good leaders need procedural clarity at this point to help the group assign tasks to committees or work groups, to initiate specific follow-through plans that will convert the decision to action.

In all four of these phases of problem-solving, leadership behavior is a strong factor in success. In no case is the appropriate behavior a "hands off" retreat. Rather it is an awareness of a useful process which must be followed, and careful action to create procedures which do so. The leader is the person who can aid the process by what he does. In many cases he may be the person presiding or the stated leader. But he could also be any member of the group with insight in analyzing what is happening and skill in seeing what next needs to be done.

Conclusion

The foregoing has mentioned only a few of the many aspects of group functioning. These can be expanded much farther and other major areas can be discovered in current writing and study going on in the field. One of the most concise analyses of groups is found in the pamphlet *Group Development*.[1]

In the field of group development, however, one learns to be an effective participant and an effective leader not just by reading books, but through training experiences. The word "training" is useful to describe the process whereby knowledge at the intellectual level becomes functional in behavior. In group process training emphasis is placed upon learning new concepts and techniques, as well as identifying one's own characteristic behavior which may not always be deliberate or visible to the individual at the conscious level.

A variety of group dynamics courses are now offered at colleges and universities in the curriculum of extension courses and in the training programs of volunteer service organizations. A number of denominations have made use of group dynamics insights in their preparation of curriculum materials and their training of leaders.

One of the focal points for training in this field has been the National Training Laboratories, an agency of the National Education Association in Washington, D.C. They offer extensive summer courses in Bethel, Maine. A variety of specialized designs have been created to provide training for persons in specific aspects of leadership, for persons in similar vocational settings, or for persons confronting identical problems. In consultation with the National Council of Churches, an annual institute has been set up specifically geared to some of the problems common to groups in church settings. They have also made trainers available to denominational groupings and Councils of Churches who desire to provide training experiences close to the local level. Any person engaged in leadership needs the stimulation of such a "refresher" if he is to be aware of his own style and to continue to grow in his own effectiveness.

A full account of the process going on in a group would require much more space than is available here. This chapter has sought, rather, to identify some of the important characteristics of behavior observable in groups, and to suggest ways in which they can be turned to productive account. An abundant literature is available for those who wish to pursue the subject in more detail. One observation must be added: no amount of *reading about* groups will turn a person into an effective group leader or member. For that, he needs actual experience under critical supervision. Only through this kind of "feedback" will he be able to see his present patterns of behavior and change them into more effective behavior.

6. Personality Changes in Groups

QUENTIN L. HAND

> Broad and sometimes extravagant claims are made for the
> changes in personal life and character resulting from partici-
> pation in interpersonal groups, particularly those called
> prayer groups. To what extent are these claims justified? In a
> research project carried on among group members in churches
> of which he was pastor, Dr. Hand undertook to measure such
> changes. While the findings are not to be generalized for all
> groups, they point significantly to the kind of study needed
> to validate any claims that are made. Quentin Hand is Asso-
> ciate Professor of Psychology and Pastoral Counseling, Candler
> School of Theology, Emory University.

"Prayer changes things." The slogan sounds good. But do
changes occur? Said one prayer group member, "We've seen
lives changed in our group." There is no doubt that group
members believe change has been effected. But is there an
observable difference in behavior? Or is there only a new
emotional tone associated with unchanged actions?

Prayer Groups versus Prayer Therapy Groups

In this chapter a distinction is made between "prayer groups"
and "prayer therapy groups" (or spiritual growth groups).

Prayer *therapy* groups are composed of persons seeking
emotional and interpersonal adjustment. The members are
aware of a psychological need for personality help. An inability to work harmoniously with others, or excessive anxiety that
torments one's life, or marital conflict are among the difficulties
which call for change. Prayer therapy group members enter the

groups for treatment and correction of their maladjustments. Such groups utilize both prayer and psychotherapeutic methods to promote change. The pastoral counselor in the group intervenes in the members' lives to stimulate healing. Hence, personality change is expected and sought through psychological methods coupled with prayer.

Prayer groups (as defined in this chapter) are composed of persons seeking to improve their relationship to God. Personality maladjustment, if present, is not a stated motivation for joining such a group. Alteration of interpersonal situations is not a major purpose. There is no planned psychotherapeutic factor in these groups. It is fellowship with God and other seekers which is sought. It is of these groups we ask, "Are persons really different when they participate in a prayer group?"

A Study of Prayer Group Participants

The information required to answer the above question accurately involves more than personal testimony. If we desire to measure change with some objectivity, we must establish a starting point and use measuring tools which others can also employ. It was such a study which the author made in a group of churches in New England.

A total of five groups were involved, with thirty persons participating. Twenty-two persons continued in the prayer groups through the test period; eight dropped out.

Each person took a battery of psychological tests, wrote a spiritual autobiography, and was interviewed before joining the group. During the existence of the group each member completed report forms of his experience and his observations of fellow members. The tests and interviews were repeated at the end of the study period. In this way, data about twenty-two of the thirty persons was collected before, during, and after participation in the prayer groups. In addition the author was present as a participant-observer in the groups, attending all meetings of three groups and occasional meetings of the other two.

Three kinds of information were sought. First, were there measurable changes in personality traits, in aspiration level, or in personal self-understanding? Second, were new patterns of social relationships developed at home, at work, or with the other prayer group members? Third, what changes occurred in religious beliefs and practices?

Are people who join prayer groups like other people? Or are they more "religious" than other people? Understanding the personality changes which occur will vary in keeping with the answer.

A summary of the characteristics of the persons in the groups studied may suggest some answer.

Most of the members were married (80%); women (73%); and in their thirties (40%). Half of them had some education beyond high school. Two-thirds of the women stated "Housewife" as their occupation. Of the sixteen employed members, three were blue-collar workers, seven worked at skilled or white-collar occupations, and six were professional people. They were a stable group in residence; eleven had lived in their homes fifteen years or more, and another ten had lived in the same home for five or more years.

As a group they are much more restrained and serious-minded than the general public. They are less aggressive toward others, and they have less drive toward accomplishment than the average person. They score as much more friendly than other Americans on a standardized test.[1]

When the prayer group participants were compared with active church workers (Official Board members, church school teachers, etc.) in the same churches, those in prayer groups had a slightly younger average age and a higher average level of educational attainment. But in terms of personality traits they showed no significant differences. In brief, prayer group members in this study differed from other active church workers chiefly in joining the prayer groups.

Some Changes Which Occurred

Twenty-two members reported on their lives during and after the prayer group experiences. Nearly all of them stated that their relationship to God had improved considerably. This was described in terms of increased assurance of God's concern for the person, of communication with God, and of the Divine presence.

All except one reported or were observed to have improved relationships with other prayer group members. Some of the manifest signs were: less anxiety with each other, increased verbal participation in meetings, fewer conventional comments, and more comments which shared personal needs or convictions. Friendships were formed among group members who previously had been casual acquaintances. Subjectively they reported that feelings of trust, warmth, and closeness for each other were generated from the prayer group experience.

Their general social relationships also showed differences. About three-fourths of them were evaluated to be more pleasant at home and/or work, to show more consideration for others, and to act with more sensitivity to others. Their own reports indicated they gave more attention to understanding and to helping others.

About half made changes in their religious beliefs; these were movements from naïve, unexamined doctrines toward more carefully examined and more clearly articulated concepts.

Fewer than one-third changed in their participation in church activities. The majority had been active in their churches; they continued to be responsible leaders. The few who showed change became more active, with one exception.

On the other hand, only three participants showed changes in their social values. For 90 percent of the group their views on social justice, racial relations, war and peace, production and distribution of wealth remained constant. In the light of the improved interpersonal relationships reported, the lack of change in social viewpoint is striking.

Only one person showed any difference in her aspiration level. She had a lower level of search for achievement after the prayer group experience.

The Most Changed Subjects

Seven of the twenty-two participants registered change in nine or more of the thirteen subcategories observed. These seven subjects showed major changes in personality, in social behavior, and in personal religious practices.

There was no one type of change in personality trait recorded. Rather, a more global pattern of personality variation occurred. These persons moved toward a more realistic evaluation of themselves. They tended to set self-ideals that were attainable, to form self-concepts that were self-respecting rather than self-depreciating. The tension between one's self-ideal and the self-concept was reduced; in religious terminology, they could forgive their own faults and accept themselves as loved by God as they were. They gained insight about their own patterns of behavior, recognizing ways of relating to others which they had previously ignored. For some, there was depth insight into the psychodynamics of their behavior in addition to the recognition of those patterns.

In their social relationships, both in the group and in daily living, these "Most Changed" subjects became more considerate of others. They reported feeling closer to members of their families and friends; they indicated a willingness to take initiative in meeting new persons and in conversations. Their behavior was in keeping with the attitudes they reported.

All seven moved to a consistent practice of personal devotions and reported a new and meaningful sense of God's presence with them. Some had questioned the reality of God; His existence now became a certainty for them.

Only two "Most Changed" participants shifted in their church activities. Both of these men had very low levels of church attendance and service before joining the prayer groups. Both became regular attendants and active church workers; both became lay speakers and accepted denominational responsibilities in addition to serving in their own congregations.

Only one "Most Changed" member showed any variation in social values. This woman began to think that disagreeing with another person was not quarreling but rather a form of respect. Hence she learned to see open disagreement between two persons as more positive than silence which ignored the difference. But the other six "Most Changed" persons had the same social values at the end of the prayer group as they had held initially.

John Redding[2] is representative of the "Most Changed" participants. He is a middle-aged, semi-skilled assembly line worker.

John was reared in a home in which a firm maternal grandfather and a strong-willed mother made the decisions. His father was an easy-going man who accepted his wife's dominance.

As a child John lived for several months with a relative. There he was permitted much freedom and few restrictions were placed on him. When he returned home his grandfather provided some discipline. But after his grandfather's death his mother's discipline was inconsistent; his father's temperament offered no firm guidance to the child. John's self-indulgence led him to pleasure-seeking companions. Soon he was a high school dropout.

He made a creditable record in military service, achieving a specialty rank of sergeant. He had done some drinking previously, and during the Second World War this became more important to him.

During the war he met and courted his wife. She was several years younger than he. John was flattered by her vision of him as a man of the world. Her adulation fed his need for approval, and his self-indulgence was served by her minimal demands of him. They were married just before he went overseas.

The years that followed his military service were hard. He was unskilled and had difficulty finding steady work. He wanted friendship and approval; he found these most easily in a tavern. His wife was ill several times, and there were medical bills reducing an uncertain income.

His drinking increased, and he began to lose jobs for absenteeism. His wife would often lie to employers that "John is sick today." He was arrested several times for drunkenness, but his mother always paid his fines. John had become an alcoholic, but he was not ready to admit it.

After John had lost several jobs, he obtained one in which his supervisor was a member of the local church. Although he was absent several times, his supervisor did not discharge him. However, the supervisor talked with the pastor about John.

John's wife became ill again. One night when John did not come home she telephoned the pastor. Thus he was at the home when John arrived in a partially drunken state. The pastor's presence, his supervisor's concern, his wife's illness, and his parent's anger all contributed to John's guilt. That night he admitted his alcoholism and asked for help.

John began a series of counseling interviews with the pastor, but these soon terminated. He joined the prayer group about two months after his request for help.

His group was studying the Bible, and he came to the sessions with commentaries and notes. After being silent for several meetings, he began to offer comments from his notes or read from commentaries. One evening another member said, "It's good to consult the experts, but what do *you* think?" The concept that he had ideas which the group valued was new and rewarding to John. He responded with more open sharing of his thoughts and experiences in following meetings.

After six months of meetings, the group reported their experiences to the congregation. John was asked by the group to be one of the two speakers.

He became a teacher in the church school, served as an usher, and was elected vice-president of the Men's Club. One year later he became president of the Men's Club and a member of the church governing body. At the time the prayer group terminated he was a district officer in the lay activities of his denomination and active at the state level also.

At home John became a more considerate husband and shared parental responsibilities of love and discipline for his children. At work he ended his absenteeism and became a more valuable employee. In his total social relationships he was a friendlier, more outgoing person; he also accepted an office in a community service organization.

The Least Changed Members

There were seven persons who showed changes in five or fewer of the thirteen subcategories. In only two categories was there similarity among these persons. Six of the seven showed improvement in their relationship to God and in their relationships with other group members.

None of the "Least Changed" developed insight into their own personalities, and only two of them changed in personality traits. Of the two, one scored higher in aggressiveness in social situations. The other showed higher scores in sociability and friendliness and a lower score in emotional stability.

The improved relationships with group members did not extend to other personal relationships. The "Least Changed" continued in the same social patterns they had used before the prayer group experience.

They also showed little difference in their religious beliefs and practices. The reported improved relationship with God did not reach into their actions. While they said they felt closer to God, only one of the seven reported any religious experience during the nine months of prayer group membership.

Ralph Garnet is representative of the "Least Changed" group. He is a slender man, short in stature, unassuming in appearance. In his fifties, he and his wife have been married about thirty years. They had one child who is now a married adult.

Ralph's father died when he was still an infant. His mother married some two years later. His stepfather was a quiet, uneducated man. He exercised kindly discipline, often taking

Ralph with him to teach him the skills of farming. Ralph's mother was a quiet, controlled woman who showed little affection.

His childhood home provided the necessities of life for Ralph but little more. The home training was moralistic and firm. Elementary education was provided in a one-room school; the nearest high school was several miles, and Ralph did not attend.

As a young man Ralph held a series of jobs that were low in status and pay. He spent three years in military service; it was after the First World War, and he did not advance in rank. After his discharge he again held a series of low-paying jobs.

He married shortly after leaving military service. He and his wife sporadically attended various churches without forming a continuing relationship to a church.

Then in the late 1940's Ralph moved his family into his present home. His wife became a member of a church women's group. When he was ill, this group sent flowers to his hospital room. Later a man from the church invited him to the men's group organizational meeting. He attended and was elected alternate secretary. When the man first chosen refused to serve, the office became his. He kept it, "in order to do my part."

From this beginning he was asked to become an usher, then a member of the governing body, and finally to work in the church school. Each new responsibility was accepted as "doing my part."

At the time the prayer group was formed Ralph joined because "as a church leader I should set a good example." During the year and a half covered by the study he was a task-oriented member. He was regular in attendance and made frequent contributions to the discussions.

Ralph's life changed somewhat during the prayer group's existence. On test scores he showed greater sociability and friendliness, but his emotional stability score dropped significantly. However, these changes of attitude were not observed in his behavior.

His relationship to other group members was described by

him as, "I feel a bit closer to them." Again this attitudinal change was not apparent to others.

Ralph had been an active church worker before joining the group and he continued to serve at this level while participating in his group. His devotional life changed very little in practices of prayer, Bible reading, or meditation. He indicated that he felt "a bit closer to God" than he had. His beliefs about God and the Christian religion remained constant.

Some Unexpected Findings

Not all personality factors apparent in the prayer groups have reference to changes. Some observations were not anticipated, but it seems appropriate to report them.

Mark was a dedicated Christian in his middle twenties. He was a college graduate who earnestly sought to increase his understanding. He could express himself well. He studied the material which his prayer group was reading, and he came to meetings with questions that perplexed him. Mark was inclined to be aggressive in taking leadership, and he was persistent in seeking answers. Several members of the group had less formal education than he had, and they tended to remain silent when Mark spoke. Both he and the others would turn to the minister for "answers" rather than use Mark's questions as a basis for mutual thought. When Mark was not given classroom-type answers, his anxious seeking was intensified. He would not accept group search and interpersonal fellowship as an alternative to authoritative answers, and Mark ended his participation at the end of four months.

Mr. and Mrs. Jones were very much like the "Least Changed" persons when they joined the prayer group. However, they remained in the group only fifteen sessions; they were absent from four of those fifteen. Mr. and Mrs. Jones were both about fifty years of age, active in their church, well established in their community as leaders. Neither had completed high school, and both were reluctant to admit this. Both of them were dependent upon others' approval to maintain their own self-esteem. Both joined the prayer group because they wanted to support the church's (and their minister's) program. They did not understand the necessity of either the personal devotional discipline or the required attendance at prayer group meetings. They waited to be instructed in the group meetings as they would have been in a church school class. Their compliance with what they thought was expected of them was insufficient to hold them as members.

Another type of personality problem was manifested by Doris. She was a plain-looking woman in her twenties. She had taken six years to complete high school, and her parents were of low socioeconomic status. She was the only girl, and her two older brothers had treated her as a boy. Thus Doris had limited intellectual and social resources to make friends and to keep them.

Doris had attended the church regularly for several months. A friend had encouraged her to join the choir; this had provided a sense of belonging and of serving which were important to her. However, Doris was tone-deaf, and the other choir members complained to the director. He attempted to provide special instruction, but her limitation made this useless. She was asked to leave the choir, which she resented.

It was at this point that Doris joined the prayer group. The same friend was again the initiator of this action. In the group Doris's ways of relating to others were more evident. She had two patterns. The first of these was to tell of her illnesses, her aches and pains, her visits to the dentist, etc., in detail. Her second pattern was to make physical contact by lightly striking the other's arm, or slapping another's back, or grasping another person's hand. Doris did not know how to participate in a group discussion or how to share attention with others.

Initially the group met Doris's need to be a member of something. Other members tried to understand and accept her. But as several meetings passed without a change in Doris, the group began to ignore her stories about sore throats and athlete's foot. They began to keep enough distance to be out of Doris's range.

Her attendance at worship services became infrequent. She reported to the group she had a boyfriend, a man several years older than she. Soon thereafter she dropped out of the prayer group and ceased participation in the church entirely. Because of her personality limitations, Doris could not give the prayer group the participation expected of her. In turn, she experienced frustration and a rejection of the group and church followed.

Another type of personality was seen in Helen. She was an attractive woman in her twenties, a college graduate who met others easily. She read widely and could exchange ideas in critical investigation and discussion. She had attended a few retreats; those had a pronounced effect upon her religious concepts.

Helen appeared confident, but much of this certainty was a cover for her doubts. She had religious doubts which were masked by vocal convictions. She had questions about her self-worth which were disguised by her college degree and her talk of many books.

The prayer group to which Helen belonged was composed of women, most of them near her age and educational attainment. Their meetings had quite active discussion, with all members commenting on the issues before them.

To the observer it was evident that Helen was the leader of the group. Her comments would summarize the discussion; at other times she initiated new topics by a casual statement. When someone disagreed with the majority, all would look toward Helen and wait for her response.

Yet, the group members did not acknowledge Helen's leadership. When group members were asked individually to designate the person who made the most contribution, or the one who spoke most frequently, or the leader of the group, the members would respond with four or five names. No group member, including Helen, recognized the part she had played in the group.

This group had twenty-six meetings over an eight-month period. About the eighteenth meeting a discussion of the nature of Christian dedication occurred. Helen found herself a minority of one in the position she presented. Previously differences had been accepted. But Helen emphatically insisted the others should change to her way of thinking. They did not, and the meeting ended angrily.

Helen missed the next two meetings; she was not present for the last two. Her interest in the group declined according to her report, and others' comments about her confirmed this. She did not recognize why she had changed, nor when.

Helen's insecurity had been allayed when others followed her lead. But she took disagreement with her ideas to be rejection of her as a person. Her need to see herself as an adequate, knowledgeable person was challenged, so withdrawal from active participation was her means of maintaining a self-image of certainty and worth.

These five members demonstrate personality factors which were magnified by prayer group participation. Four of them were adequate and effective in their daily living. In family and community relationships their patterns of behavior were satisfactory. But in the intensity of the small group interaction their personality traits conflicted with group expectations. The results were unsatisfactory to the persons themselves and to the prayer groups.

Psychological Factors in Personality Change

While the study tried to document personal change in an objective manner, interest in the psychological factors was also present. Some suggestive statements can be made.

The amount of personal change experienced was related to age, occurring more significantly among younger members. The "Most Changed" group also averaged more years of formal education than the "Least Changed."

Motivation for joining the prayer groups also was related to personality change. Some joined because they desired to change their lives or have new experiences. For example, one member said, "I've never been quite certain about God, and I want to find out if He will respond." Others joined because they wished to continue religious practices they had or to maintain their lives as they were. A woman, representative of this group, said, "I've always prayed. One can never pray too much." As might be anticipated, those whose motives for joining were chiefly expansive showed more change than those with maintenance motives.

Another factor related to personality change was the relationship to the group leader. One prayer group member who wanted to be like Helen ended with more self-doubt and lower self-esteem. A member of another group was encouraged in her growth by the leader. John Redding used his relationship to his pastor (the effective leader of that group) to aid in the extensive changes he achieved.

The acceptance or rejection of a member by the group was another factor associated with personal change. The rejection of Doris and of Helen contributed to their loss of interest. The group expected John Redding to make changes in his life, and he did. The group to which Ralph Garnet belonged accepted his active participation in the church, and he was not expected to change.

The practice of daily devotions was not related to personality change. All prayer group participants had times of prayer and Bible reading daily. Almost all of them felt this was significant to them. But the content of the devotional periods was quite similar for "Most Changed" and "Least Changed" and "Drop Out" members.

The reader may well ask why no reference has been made to the grace of God in personality change. This has been for two reasons. First, the grace of God can not be measured by the tools employed in this study. Hence there is no objective means of reporting its presence in the life of a subject. Second, the writer assumes that God uses many methods for His work in human life. Hence, when two or three were gathered in His name, then the grace of God was present. It is assumed that grace was in the various factors suggested.

Concluding Thoughts

While this chapter has dealt with personality change, prayer groups should not be evaluated solely on the basis of such changes. That is, one should not value a group highly just because several members show changes. Neither should a group in which few or no members change in personal characteristics be counted a failure.

In one group studied there was a member who made no changes. During the year she had several crises in her life, including the death of a parent and of her husband, critical illness in a grandchild, and serious illness of her own. She stated that without the group she could not have maintained her sanity. The writer was inclined to see her self-evaluation as realistic; the group was a very important help and strength to that member. The support they gave to her made the group worthwhile, even though she did not show personality change.

The deliberate attempt to use prayer groups for personality change can be dangerous from both psychological and theological perspectives.

When prayer groups are used to effect changes, one is entering the realm of psychotherapy. Those who practice either psychotherapy or intensive counseling know that extensive training is necessary. When the poorly trained person intervenes in the life of another, he may cause more damage than growth. When a minister or other prayer group member tries to use a prayer group as a substitute for psychotherapy, he may be opening wounds in others or himself.

A therapy group, conducted by a well-trained pastoral counselor, which employs prayer in its conduct is a different matter. Reference has been made to such groups elsewhere in this book.

There are also theological objections to use of prayer groups to create personality change. This would treat God as a device or power to be employed at our bidding. Prayer, in such a group, would become a magical incantation to bring about change. The communication between God and man would be reduced to God's giving and man's getting of personality adjustment.

Members of prayer groups do change. There is objective evidence to corroborate the anecdotal material often read. When persons seek to live in fellowship with God, growth occurs for some. Regression occurs for others. But constant self-examination for the signs of change will short-circuit the fellowship with God. Rather let the prayer group member seek first God and His kingdom, and then growth will come as well.

7. Preaching and Small Groups

CLYDE REID

> Preaching as the church's way of communicating the Gospel
> and small groups as arenas of dialogue are sometimes re-
> garded as competitive. Dr. Reid finds this antithesis unjusti-
> fied. His study of the relationship between participation in
> groups and response to the sermon suggests a strongly com-
> plementary function for each. Formerly on the faculty of
> Union Theological Seminary, and the staff of the Department
> of Evangelism of the United Church of Christ, Clyde Reid
> is now Associate Director of the Institute for Advanced Pas-
> toral Studies. He is author of *The God-Evaders, The Empty
> Pulpit,* and articles in religious journals, and a trainer in
> group conferences and workshops.

What is the relationship between small groups and preaching?
Will small groups replace the sermon as the primary vehicle
for the communication of the Gospel, as some suggest? [1] Or is
there another possibility—that small groups and preaching can
actually strengthen each other in a partnership? I am convinced that preaching and small groups can be allies.

In fact, there is considerable evidence which suggests that
membership in a small group influences an individual's responsiveness to preaching. This chapter reports the findings of a
research project to test this hypothesis. This research revealed
that the church member who regularly attends a small, personal group in which he can discuss his faith is a more deeply
involved listener on Sunday morning.

Two clues led me to zero in on the important relationship
between preaching and small groups. I first began to suspect

that there must be such a relationship when I began to explore the field of communication theory. Communications researchers were beginning to emphasize the importance of two-way communication. Where there is a two-way flow of information, or feedback, they say, the accuracy of the message is enhanced. When an individual has an opportunity to ask questions and express doubts, there is an increased possibility that he will understand the message. This led to the obvious assumption that if we really want to communicate the Gospel, we need to build feedback opportunities, or two-way communication, into the life of the church.

I found the second clue in John Casteel's book *Spiritual Renewal Through Personal Groups,* published in 1957. The book contains reports from a number of writers on small group ventures in church life. Thomas M. Steen wrote that as a result of his experience with small groups in his church, "a new depth and vitality" had been born in his preaching. He reported further that there was "more of true listening to the sermon because I am preaching with them and not for or at them." [2] A member of another church reported in the same volume that as a result of his group experience, "Now I find in worship and preaching what has been there all the time, but which now speak to *me*." [3] John Casteel himself wrote, "I am quite sure that there is a deep relation between preaching and such means of life in the church as the small groups represent. Everywhere one encounters these groups one discovers that there is an influence exerted by them on the preaching that goes on in the church." [4]

Beginning with these two clues—one dealing with the nature of communication and the other with personal experience—I developed a project to test the relationship between preaching and small groups.

Preaching and Communication

We begin with the basic assumption that preaching is an attempt to communicate. If preaching is communication, then it must be subject to the laws of human communication. It seems only natural, then, to turn to the fertile field of communication research and theory in an effort to understand how preaching can be more effective communication.

Of course there are those who claim that when a man preaches, his words take on an exalted significance. "The preacher's words become more than human speech, and God speaks through him." I do not wish to deny that God's Holy Spirit can use any human instrument. At the same time, I think we need to recognize that to elevate preaching too high may be only an escape from the rigors of judging preaching by human standards. In my experience, God tends to use natural conditions and ordinary human relationships to reveal himself; He rarely resorts to "magical" methods which escape human detection.

What is communication? It is helpful when considering this problem to remember that the word "communication" is based on the Latin *communis*, common. A leading researcher in the field of mass communications, Wilbur Schramm, has said that "When we communicate, we are trying to establish a 'commonness' with someone. That is, we are trying to share information, an idea, or an attitude . . ." [5] When we speak of communicating the Gospel, then, we are speaking of the effort to establish a commonness with someone in regard to some aspect of the Christian faith.

Until about 1950, communications researchers thought of communication chiefly as a simple, one-way process. A communicator transmitted a message to an audience with a particular effect. This approach was typified by the formula: WHO says WHAT to WHOM with what EFFECT. Since 1950, however, there has been an increasing tendency to recognize that communication is a more complex, dynamic two-way relationship, modified by many situational factors including primary group relationships, opinion leaders, and other variables. This transition has been described as a shift from the "one-way" or "transmission belt" theory of communication to a "two-way" theory.

Another crucial development in the field of communication research is consistent with the two-way theory of communication and takes it a step further. There has been an increasing tendency to distinguish a number of steps in the communication process. It is one thing simply to hear a message, and quite another to accept that message for one's own and begin acting upon it. Communications experts are now speaking of communication as the completed process. One report put it this way: "The ultimate in communication is only achieved, however, when the interacting parties understand each other, can identify with each other's point of view, and a transfer of meaning has taken place that *influences conduct*" [6] [my italics].

This understanding of communication is consistent with current definitions of preaching. Preaching is often referred to as a "summons to action" or an effort to change lives. For this reason, the distinction is crucially important to our examination of preaching and small groups.

Communications researchers now distinguish a series of steps in the communication process, and my own effort to integrate and elaborate upon these steps includes seven phases:

1. *Transmission* occurs when the communicator presents his message (or delivers his sermon).
2. *Contact* occurs when the listener has heard the message.
3. When the listener is allowed to ask a question, make a comment, or otherwise express himself concerning the message, *feedback* is established and there is a beginning of dialogue.
4. *Comprehension.* Having clarified his understanding of the message, the listener now comprehends what it is the communicator is trying to say to him.
5. *Acceptance.* Having understood the message, the listener now accepts, ignores, or rejects it. His prior beliefs and attitudes, his relationships with influential persons, and his primary group relationships may modify his acceptance or rejection of the message.
6. *Internalization.* Beyond simply accepting the message intellectually, the listener internalizes it when it becomes his own, a part of his own being, and begins to influence his behavior.
7. *Action.* At this level, the communicator and listener (who has

also become a communicator in the two-way process) have a common, shared understanding and are *acting* on the basis of this understanding. This is what communications researchers are now calling *complete communication.* "A transfer of meaning has taken place which influences conduct."

Communication research increasingly points to the need for feedback or two-way communication in those instances when we expect comprehension, acceptance, internalization, and action to take place. Monologue is rarely enough if we desire genuine communication; a two-way flow of information is almost essential. In our preaching efforts, we tend to rely heavily on one-way communication, assuming that nothing more is necessary in order to accomplish the goal of shared meaning. We have been satisfied simply to make contact with our listeners, assuming that this is sufficient. After all, it is threatening to hear feedback and discover that our leading laymen have neither understood us nor accepted what we have been preaching for years. Monological communication is safer.

This absence of dialogue in the preaching situation may be the key to understanding the failure of preaching to achieve the results in changed lives which we have always claimed for it.

An active layman once told me of his concern about preaching. He said, "You hear just so many sermons and you have so many questions you would like to ask that you quit listening; it goes in one ear and out the other." He was expressing in classic form the results of monological communication, when no opportunity is provided for the listener to express himself and participate in the dialogue.

In his book *The Miracle of Dialogue,* Reuel L. Howe has pointed out that many people naïvely believe that communication takes place simply by telling people "what they ought to know." He speaks of this as the "monological illusion," and comments out of his experience with the Institute for Advanced Pastoral Studies that "young ministers are disillusioned about the effectiveness of preaching and suspect that 'telling' is not a sure means of communication, but because they know of no alternative they are caught in the one-way street of monologue." [7]

If communication requires dialogue, and if small groups provide that dialogue, it seemed reasonable to me that small groups should strengthen the preaching effort. I set out to test that hypothesis through field research in a number of churches where small groups formed a vital part of church life.

Dialogue in Small Groups

To test my conviction that small group dialogue should strengthen preaching, I first conducted a broad survey to discover how many churches were using small groups in a given area of New England. I also wanted to know what types of groups were current.[8]

To my surprise, nearly 50 per cent of the churches reporting indicated that they had some type of small groups active. Bible study groups were the largest single category, far outnumbering prayer groups, study groups, or sermon discussion groups. Sixteen per cent of the churches reported some sermon discussion, but less than 10 per cent had an ongoing sermon discussion pattern. It was my feeling, however, that actual sermon discussion was not the crucial thing. Any small group which meets regularly for Bible study, prayer, or discussion provides an indirect dialogue with the minister's preaching and strengthens his efforts to communicate the Gospel. If dialogue is actually established, then members of such groups should reveal a deeper involvement in the preached Word and in the life of the church as a result of their group experience.

That this hypothesis is actually true was demonstrated by the second phase of the research project. A more intensive survey of 105 members of twelve Bible study, prayer, and sermon discussion groups revealed that participation in such a group does result in an increased responsiveness to preaching. Members of the twelve groups filled out questionnaires in which they indicated their feelings about the group experience, ten of the groups were visited by the researcher, and ten of the ministers were interviewed about their feelings.

One interesting finding of the research was the value of the group experience to the ministers. Nine of the ten ministers interviewed testified that their sermon preparation had been influenced by the feedback gained through the group process. The other minister did not meet with the groups personally, so could not report this result. The ministers also reported that they knew their people and their needs better as a result of the group experience.

The 105 group members interviewed were asked three carefully constructed and closely related questions to evaluate the relationship between their group participation and preaching.[9] On these three questions, the 105 respondents scored a high average, indicating a strong, positive relationship between group participation and responsiveness to preaching. Nearly three-fourths reported some increase or much increase in their ability to understand the sermon. A majority reported that their minister's sermons spoke to their condition more or much more than before, and nearly 75 per cent indicated that their interest and attention, or sensitivity, during the preaching of the sermon were more or much more than before joining a group.

In addition, approximately one-fourth of the group members with room for improvement in their attendance reported an increase in their Sunday worship due to their group affiliation. The same percentage reported that they increased their leadership activity in the church due to group membership. Some sample comments by group members follow:

> This group provides an anvil on which to pound out what one believes; I believe that my own faith has been strengthened, or established, by what we do in the group . . .

> I think I have learned more in one year than in all the years of church attendance.

> I feel that belonging to this group, acquiring the attitudes and feeling the closeness of God contributes greatly to my ability to

worship at the church service on Sunday. My attention wanders less and I am more "at one" with God during the service.

One of the significant differences which was revealed by the analysis of the data from this survey was related to length of time in a group. Those who had been members of a group for two years or more scored significantly higher than those who had been members for less than two years, indicating that length of time in a group is an important factor in the relationship to preaching sensitivity. This would explain why some of the efforts to program small groups meet with disappointment; the programmers may be looking for results too soon.

To summarize, the research project demonstrated that participation in a small group where a two-way flow of communication on the content of the Gospel takes place does influence the way in which the group members respond to preaching. This finding is consistent with the findings of research on communication, which increasingly emphasize the importance of feedback and two-way flow if communication is to be complete or reach the action level.

Other Conditions

In addition to the length-of-time element just mentioned, there are two other dimensions which are worthy of further mention. The first is leadership style. At this point, I leave the sure ground of a carefully researched area and launch into the realm of speculation. Solid research on leadership styles for small groups remains to be done. However, from what we know of leadership research and theory, it is possible to reach several tentative conclusions. In general, an authoritarian style of leadership, in which one person does most of the speaking and decision making, would militate against free and open communication. Far more appropriate to the small group, and more consistent with the principle of two-way communication, is the shared leadership approach. In this approach, the leadership of the group is supplied by various group members, rather than being centered in one person. If our goal is open discussion, in which group members share in the discussion of the Gospel, then shared leadership is almost certainly to be preferred.

This research project did not yield any helpful data on the value of leadership styles. The nine ministers involved with groups in their churches tended to use widely varying leadership styles. Since the research did not focus on this dimension and the samples were so small, no firm results can be reported. However, some obvious questions call out for further research.

Preaching is basically an authoritarian style of leadership. The decision-making machinery is focused in one man. Is there a contradiction involved when the same minister uses the authoritarian preaching style to address his people on Sunday, but works with them on the basis of a more democratic leadership style at other times? Or can he modify his preaching style to reflect an attitude of shared, democratic leadership? We do not have enough data to answer these questions, but one speculation may be safely offered.

From what we now know of leadership theory, very few persons can carry off the leadership pattern in which the charismatic leader wins a large following by asserting his authority dogmatically. The old-style preacher figure who had all the answers just won't work in most places today. A new leadership style is required and is emerging. This same principle should apply to the minister's leadership of small groups. The democratic style, which frees the shared leadership of the entire group, should produce more fruits of creativity than an autocratic approach. Careful research in the future will allow us to make more definite statements on this matter.

The other condition of group life to which attention should be paid is that of the communication level. Some authorities distinguish levels of communication in groups, beginning with a fairly superficial level marked by rational discussion, advice-giving, and the avoidance of personal feelings. The second level is more personal and less rational, with more emotional content.[10] My research on groups indicated that when communication tended to reach a more personal level, a greater influence on preaching sensitivity was recorded. Many elements influence the level of trust present in a group, which determines how much group members may share personal material with each other. The importance of this finding is that it suggests the value in group leaders helping to create a structure in which personal sharing may emerge in an atmosphere of trust. When a group is structured to prevent anything but superficial discussion of ideas, it may be less effective in providing a deep feedback effect.

The Missing Link

What, then, may we say in conclusion about the relationship between preaching and small groups in the life of the church? The one fact that emerges with clarity is the value of small groups in strengthening the minister's task of communicating the Gospel. Participation in a small group may be understood as providing the missing link for preaching, the feedback link that allows a deeper personal response to the sermon. Preaching and small groups may work in a partnership relation; they should not be seen as rival modes of communication. How is this possible? Several facts stand out.

1. When a minister participates in the small group program himself, he finds that he learns to know his people and their needs more intimately, and this knowledge helps him to "aim" his sermons more accurately to meet these needs. It provides him with a listening post, apart from personal growth benefits he shares with other group members. The real questions, doubts, and concerns of his people can then strengthen his preaching efforts, and keep them grounded in reality.

2. The preaching effort may be enfeebled because of the lack of two-way communication, according to current theory in the field of communication. The small group provides the layman with an opportunity to express his doubts and his questions, supplying a feedback link with the minister's efforts to communicate the Gospel. This can happen when the purpose of

the group is specifically to discuss the sermon, but it can also happen when the group is organized around a Bible study focus, or as a prayer group or study group. The key seems to be the importance of the group in providing an open discussion opportunity on the *content* of the Gospel, and one's personal response to that message. Too often, preaching merely makes contact with the listener, whereas a discussion process allows the message to reach deeper communication levels with greater potentiality of influencing action.

3. The preaching situation does not provide the average layman or lay woman with a deep feeling of involvement. When that person has opportunity to speak as well as listen, to be heard as well as to hear another, he feels that his personhood is more deeply involved. More of him is invested in the life and work of the institution as a result.

4. The small group experience, by providing the individual with an opportunity to speak, gives him a greater sense of worth. His point of view is taken into account; his ideas are responded to. As a result, his dignity as a person is enhanced.

5. For many group members, the Gospel comes alive in their group experience for the first time. In their small group, they actually experience the accepting, forgiving love of their fellow church members, whereas they had only heard of this love from the pulpit before. They find personal support in a family crisis, help in making a crucial vocational decision, or the expression of love when death comes near in the hospital. Because these experiences bring new life to such Christian terms as acceptance, love, and *koinonia,* the sermon takes on new life and depth. The message can now be heard and understood because it touches depths of reality in the listener's experience. This is perhaps the most important point at which small groups strengthen the pulpit ministry.

Rather than being seen as a rival or threat to pulpit communication, the small group movement should be welcomed as a partner and ally.

8. The Counseling Group

JOSEPH W. KNOWLES

The term "therapy" is often used with considerable inexactness in accounts of group goals and experience. In this chapter, Joseph Knowles, Th. D., clarifies its meaning by describing the aims, procedures, and qualifications of participants and of the leader in groups that can be accurately called therapeutic. He draws upon wide experience in the pastorate, as Director of the Baptist Counseling Service in Los Angeles, and professor at the Institute of Religion, Houston, Texas. Author of *Group Counseling,* in the Successful Pastoral Counseling Series, he is now Pastoral counseling specialist at the Church of the Saviour, Washington, D.C.

Many churches today are concerned with the possibilities of group counseling as a method by which to meet the growing need of persons for support, counseling, and guidance. Now the time has come when this area requires careful definition and clear treatment as to its possibilities, procedures, leadership, and dangers. The following discussion attempts this kind of clarification.

Viewed in perspective, the roots of group counseling and group psychotherapy go far back in recorded time to the use of a group approach to influence and change human behavior. However, Joseph H. Pratt, a Boston physician, receives credit as the first person to make use of the group method for scientific treatment purposes. In 1905 Pratt gathered slum-tubercular patients together to instruct them concerning hygiene, diet, and medications; and employed inspirational methods to sustain patients' morale. Interestingly enough, Pratt's colleagues were skeptical of his endeavors, but he found financial support and personal encouragement from the Emmanuel Episcopal Church and its minister, Reverend Elwood Worchester. Another pioneer in group treatment methods, L. Cody Marsh (1928), was a minister who became a psychiatrist. It is not surprising, therefore, that the church with its recognition of the healing potential in corporate life of community should play a role in the discovery and scientific application of the group method of therapy.

How a Counseling Group Is Set Up

A counseling group differs in many ways from other small groups. How a counseling group is set up—its purpose, duration, size, composition, and contract between members and leader—makes its difference apparent. Essential to any fully functional group is clarity as to *purpose* and *commitment* on the part of members to that purpose. A counseling group is set up to assist persons with conflictual difficulties in living. These conflicts are of sufficient severity and duration to interfere significantly with growth, functioning, and fulfillment in one or more areas of personal identity, vocation, social relationships, dating or marriage, or loss of faith and meaning in life. This means that individuals in a counseling group have already recognized and acknowledged a need for help and come into a group motivated by the desire to discover the source of their dis-ease and to experiment with more fruitful modes of being, believing, and behaving.

Group members, therefore, early recognize and foster this therapeutic purpose. They test the motivation and purpose of any new member. Among the first questions directed to a new member may be, "Why are you here? Do you have problems?" Occasionally a member will say, "We don't want you here if you do not have problems. It's too painful to talk of my suffering in the presence of a person who seems to have no difficulties." Reference to the group as "a class" gets challenged. Also, if a person talks of enjoying the group or relates only his successes and joys, members move into the question of whether the person really needs to be in counseling. In other words, a counseling group is structured as a time and place where it is appropriate and expected that people will have opportunity and freedom to share with others the dark things of the soul.

The purpose of the counseling group calls for a unique *contract* or *covenant* on the part of members and leader. For trust and spontaneous communication to develop, members commit themselves to regard all group events as privileged, confidential communication. Group transactions are not discussed with nongroup members, not even a spouse. One is free, of course, to discuss himself with a nonmember. Furthermore, a member is asked to bring to the group significant conversation with another member so that "draining off" does not happen outside the group.

Fees, too, are a part of the contract, if they are charged. Fees may be necessary to pay for the services of a pastoral counseling specialist, but primarily, charging fees has therapeutic implications. For example, fees free the person from a sense of obligation, so that he may make use of the counselor's time without guilt and be free to say and feel what he needs to experience. Fees also motivate the counselee to make responsible use of the experience for personal growth. Fees help avoid fostering dependency in which the person is on the receiving end as though he had no responsibility or nothing to give in the relationship. Fees also place professional and ethical responsibility upon the counselor to give help. As a part of their contractual arrangement, fees therefore foster responsibility in both the counselor and the counselee.

Finally, each member alerts the group a week in advance of any thoughts of leaving. He agrees to come an additional time to allow one week to test his decision to leave and to have assistance in the evaluation.

Group purpose and covenant then become selective factors in the choice of group members. *Group composition* is another selective principle. Again the counseling group differs from most other small groups in that members are chosen by the leader. This choice is necessary to ensure a high level of interaction between members. Ideally, any group should have some balance between various role behaviors of members. For example, interaction is facilitated when a group includes the more active participants as well as observers; the forward and the retiring; the vocal and the less vocal; the more emotional and the more analytical; the more impulsive and the more restrained; and the more nurturing and comforting ones as over against those who tend to confront and advise. Each brings his diverse gifts to make the group more fully functional.

The leader may form a group on either the basis of heterogeneity or homogeneity. Heterogeneous groups further amplify the principle of difference. Here the leader includes persons of both sexes; the single, married, widowed, and divorced; ages ranging from twenty-two to fifty-five; and differences of social class, racial, ethnic, religious, and educational backgrounds. However, each person should have at least one other person with whom he can feel a sense of empathy and whom he can count on for support.

Homogeneous groups emphasize the aspect of similarity or commonality between members. Here grouping is made according to sex, age, or a common problem. One may begin a group exclusively for men or women; for any age group ranging from adolescents to the aged; or to deal with a common problem such as marriage conflict, alcoholism, or obesity. For example, one of the author's groups is for single, young adult women who are interested in becoming married as well as in their own personal growth.

In some instances several persons may sense the need for counseling to facilitate their personal and spiritual growth. They may form a group and secure the assistance of a qualified leader. The leader may be a minister with specialized training in counseling who is either on the church staff or who is known by the group. In many metropolitan communities a group can find social workers, counseling psychologists, marriage counselors, or psychiatrists who are interested in work with church groups. One disadvantage of the group's forming itself lies in the fact that these persons often are friends. Their social involvement may limit the depth of their interaction with one another. Too, such groups often exclude disliked persons whose presence in the group can be an asset.

Counseling groups are limited as to the number of members. Eight to ten persons provide sufficient interactional roles, yet allow time and opportunity for each to avail himself of the benefits of the group. Some groups meet more than once each week; however, meetings generally are once weekly for ninety minutes to two hours.

When does a group terminate? Some groups are structured with an end point of nine to twelve months. Other groups are continuous. When one person leaves a continuous group, a new member is brought in to fill the vacated position and role. The continuous group, therefore, has no terminal point. Members terminate when they have derived maximal benefits.

How long do individuals remain in such a group? This varies according to the depth and range of need, motivation and goal of each. Many continue for two to three years or more. Why so long? The learning and re-education process often requires it. Consideration of the group process makes this evident.

How the Group Functions

Discussion of this complex and dynamic phenomenon must of necessity be limited, but should include two basic concepts: Group Process and Group Goals. Process refers to the interaction in the immediacy of face-to-face relationships where growth and change are incited. Goals refer to what participants hope to realize in the address and response of their relationships. The goal broadly designated is to become persons—to be and become a self-in-community.

The process of therapy takes place both within the individual and between group members. This process should not be conceived, however, as limited to the formal meetings of the group. The process begun in the group spreads to encompass the larger arena of one's living—home, work, social and church relationships. These are brought into the context of therapy and used for growth, awareness, insight, and for opportunity to experiment with more fulfilling modes of communicating and relating.

While in the group, the person faces in many directions of his relational experiences in time and place. Usually one begins with a focus upon *problems encountered in the present life situation,* such as difficulties with a spouse, children, job, or current dissatisfactions or disappointments with oneself. At the onset, the group is experienced as a *peer* group of concerned persons with whom one's problems can be discussed. Trust develops as one risks himself and finds that he is heard, understood, and appreciated for his presence and communication. Confessional moments occur in which one shares the pain and guilt of failure to be the person one is called to be. Each registers surprise that he is accepted and that the group does not confirm his own self-condemnation and self-rejection. And one finds that even those aspects of himself—his anger, stubbornness, dominance, or anxiety, fear and hurt—come to be appreciated. These qualities evoke reactions that enable other members to be aware of and examine their responses.

Also, as a member observes and listens, he discovers that his problems are not uniquely different. He begins to feel more a part of the human race rather than an "oddball." One learns, too, from others who share their successes and failures in problem-solving.

While the above gifts of the group have healing import, the *reality situation* of the group provides the core value for cognitive and emotional re-education. Over against the reality and truth within the group, one can test out the validity of his feelings, values, and beliefs. Members are committed to honest communication and to respond to what each really feels and thinks. Honest communication brings to light the way in which one may misconstrue others and deceive oneself.

How one misconstrues the reality of others becomes clear because group members, at first experienced as peers, are now transformed and put in other roles. For example, a woman may find herself either hurt or angry with a male member. As this transaction is examined, she begins to see that she is reacting to the male member as she does to her husband. Or another person may transform a younger member into a son or daughter. There may or may not be similarities to the husband, son, or daughter. In such an instance the opportunity is present for each involved in the transaction to examine what is within and between each that creates such antagonism, hurt, and alienation.

One not only confronts the present and its opportunities and dilemmas; he also *faces and relives the past.* In two ways it becomes apparent that the style of life in the present has rootage in the soil of the past. First, discussion of conflicts of the present evokes memories of past achievement and difficulties. This journey into the past leads to a recovery and working through of painful memories that have been "blotted out." The pain and conflict, however, may remain. Some persons have difficulty recalling many events that occurred before adolescence.

Another way one lives his way into his past grows out of *his restructuring the peer group into the primary family* into which he was born and reared. Other members become invested with the roles of father, mother, siblings, or significant relatives. Here one moves to a more elemental level which influences how he images others and relates to them. Group transactional theory holds that one's family—living or deceased—lives within each person. The past is yet alive and active in the present. Significant past relationships have been internalized. They belong to the structure and dialogue of the inner life. One's behavior may, for example, be adversely as well as beneficially influenced and directed by a living or deceased father's or mother's expectations, beliefs, and emotionality.

These primal relationships may provide the pattern for present relationship and be a major factor at work to determine whom one selects to admit to his inner circle of acquaintances. The old song, "I want a girl just like the girl that married dear old dad," or, frequently, "I don't want such a girl," witnesses to this human proclivity. The individual therefore brings his past as well as present relationships to the group. In this reality situation he relives, reevaluates, and reshapes his mode of viewing, experiencing, and valuing.

Granted that, in the group, members repeat the dramas of contemporary and past modes of perceiving, feeling, and responding—how are these transactions converted into therapeutic gain for the participants? The fact that the old style of life recurs in a counseling group is nothing new. These behaviors are the very reason individuals sought help in the first place. What factors are present in a counseling group that are absent elsewhere? The *insight, skill,* and *experiences* of the *counselor* compose one factor. The counselor has sufficient awareness and training to detect what George Bach, a group psychotherapist, calls "set up operations." [1]

As we have seen, members set one another up and expect the other to act, think, or feel in a specific way, or believe the other is behaving in a special way with specific reference to him. For example, one set up operation is known as *projection.* Projection occurs when one attributes motives, feelings, and ideas to another, when actually this is the way the one doing the projecting actually feels or thinks. Jesus gets at this in the Sermon on the Mount when he teaches, "Judge not." Often one's judgment of another is the condemned, unacceptable, unconscious contents of one's own spirit. *Externalizations* are similar in that a member senses and talks of the problem of another without recognizing the similarity of this problem to his own. *Distortions* are operations in which one believes another has feelings toward him which he really does not have. *Transferences* occur when one acts toward a member as though he were a significant person in the family in which he grew up. Finally, *countertransferences* happen as a member accepts the role that another puts him in and acts out that role in the relationship. For example, if an individual puts a woman member in a mother role and she "mothers" him or her, this represents a countertransference.

The counselor, from his more expert and objective stance, is able to identify these operations and calls on the group to examine what is taking place. This analysis of group interactions leads members to become aware of their "interpersonal operations." Gradually members use their awareness to call attention to what is going on. Members, themselves, engage in the responsible task of bringing reality to bear in the group. Each member begins to develop some expertness in therapeutic intervention and analysis. As their awareness of interpersonal phenomena increases, they resist being imaged in a way that violates their own sense of reality as to who they are. They also contest unrealistic expectation and demands being made on them. They call upon each other to recognize otherness and uniqueness while at the same time respecting and caring for the person they oppose.

The Inward Journey

We have been obliquely considering one of the goals of members while we looked at group process. This is the *outward thrust* or the journey into community. This focuses upon the interpersonal aspects of group process and goal. Spacially and relationally, this is the world between persons. Now we turn to the *inward thrust* or the *journey into the self*. Group process makes it possible for one to confront himself in the meeting with group members. In the experience of coming to know the other in his concreteness, uniqueness, and otherness, one also comes to know himself. He faces not only neighbor; his neighbor causes him to discover his own reality and uniqueness. The neighbor evokes or calls him forth and helps him to become aware of his own separateness, difference, and distinctiveness.

This inward and outward journey hopefully leads to the *renewal* and *transformation of the self*. How does this happen? In the group situation one is faced with doing again the work of the self in its pilgrimage toward wholeness. Several words are now to be used that begin with the prefix *re-*. This suggests that what the person has already done must be done again;

but this time more affectively in the group's healing climate.

We have already pointed out that one *relives* or *re-experiences* past, present, and anticipated future events. This reliving leads to a re-discovery of who one was, is, or desires to be. Such experiencing extends the boundaries of one's awareness of himself—his feelings, thoughts, and acts. Also the person begins to *re-appraise* or *re-evaluate* his feelings, values, and relationships. For example, events in life cannot be changed. How one feels about them can change! How one sees and values himself and others may take on deeper dimension and richer color and hues.

Furthermore, one may discover that his values in life are more life-denying than appreciative of life and life-affirming. This all leads to a *re-imaging of oneself*. So often one's self-image excludes more of the reality of one's self than it includes. Often the self-image actually distorts and caricatures the reality of the person. A beautiful woman may feel that she is ugly and unattractive. A brilliant individual may feel he or she is "stupid" or intellectually inferior. Thus a person with great potentiality and gifts may not be aware of these because of the faulty self-image. In a similar fashion one may overestimate himself and what he is or should be. Superiority feelings often conceal a basic sense of inadequacy. Also high, unrealistic expectations of oneself produce inferiority feelings. One can never measure up.

In the next place, the journey into the self calls for a *reconciliation* of opposites within one's self. Often people believe that life can be only one way. They strive for a consistency that seeks to deny and eliminate the multi-faceted richness and divergences of the inner life. One learns to accept his anger as well as his love, his "blue" times as well as his joyous times, his times of distance as well as times of closeness. He learns to be and stand in who he is at the moment, knowing that the next moment, next day, or next week he may feel or think somewhat differently. Hence, one becomes free to accept the opposites in oneself and to experience them not as conflictual but as complementary.

Along with the reconciling process is also one of *re-integra-tion* or the *re-centering* of the self. Often one's values represent the code of the culture or of other significant persons. These values have not grown out of the whispering of the inner spirit that sometimes become shouts when denied. The shout is the sickness, pain and suffering. As one is enabled to listen to the stirring of his own spirit—his real wishes and hopes—a new inner core of meanings and values evolves which is integral to who the person really is, what his potentialities and limits are, and what he feels his life situation realistically asks of him. It is this new inner core of values and meanings which becomes the embodiment of what the person truly feels he is called to be and do. Though his moods and fortunes change, his life becomes ordered, stabilized, and sustained amid change in the life-long journey to fulfill his vocation and destiny. This is what we mean as we talk of re-integration. Implied also is not only the re-ordering of the self but its *re-direction*. The new vision of the self—its possibilities, call, and destiny—gives courage and inspiration to decide, to act, to fulfill the vision. One becomes less a "house divided within" and more wholehearted and singlehearted as to direction.

To summarize, the group process makes possible two journeys—the inward and the outward. The inward journey refers to confrontation with oneself. This can lead to the discovery, the re-centering and re-direction of self based upon new awareness, new meaning, and values. These meanings and values are integral because they are forged in the fires of one's experience of who he is and whom he feels called to be.

The outward journey is the task of re-relating one's self to the world of persons and things. Here one learns, as Martin Buber puts it, to stand within oneself and to respond out of who one uniquely is. He experiences his own separateness and distance. Yet at the same time, he is able to be in relation, to meet his other, to perceive and allow the other to be who he is, to allow himself to be addressed, to seek to hear the word of another's address, and to respond with his own truth.

The goal toward which the process of the group moves is

then to aid persons in their quest for wholeness and authenticity, which means to be and become a self-in-community.

The Group Counselor: His Qualifications and Task

The counselor's competence, knowledge, and skill are crucial to the process of therapy. His interpersonal competence is one essential qualification. Interpersonal competence is grounded in the emotional health of the counselor himself. To counsel others effectively, one must possess an awareness of the inner workings of his own spirit. He must be able to listen to and attend his own feelings and thoughts, as well as those of others. He needs to know (and be aware) when he is threatened, and what threatens him, in order to admit to himself his own limitations and possess the freedom that acceptance of them brings, rather than deny them or have to protect himself in distorted ways.

Interpersonal competence includes also the gift and skill of being open to another, of being able to sense what another is feeling, and put oneself in the shoes of another. Martin Buber calls this "making another present by imaging the real." On the basis of one's own experience plus listening carefully to the experience of another, one is able realistically to imagine how it is with another. Effective counseling depends on being able to stand within oneself and at the same time to enter the world of the other. This is the participant-observer relationship. One becomes subjectively participant and present, yet objectively observer, maintaining distance.

The participant stance provides that emotional safety and acceptance which the group needs in order to explore threatening feelings and ideas. The observer stance provides the necessary objectivity so that when the group becomes subjectively immersed, a "lifeguard" is present to help members to "the surface and the shore."

Other counselor qualifications include two kinds of knowledge and skill. The first is knowledge of personality development, health, illness, and the dynamics involved. The second is knowledge of therapeutic methods, and process and skill in use of this knowledge. This knowledge is acquired and skill developed in at least four ways: (1) One's own personal reading and research; (2) supervised training in the counseling of others; (3) personal psychotherapy; and (4) continuing education through a qualified consultant with whom one can discuss ongoing counseling work.

The *task* of the group counselor begins with a screening interview with each potential group member. He becomes acquainted with the person and his present understanding of his problems. The counselor may briefly explore the developmental history of the individual, for this often casts light on his style of life and how it originated. In the initial interview, the counselor determines whether the person can utilize group counseling. Usually a simple criterion is that persons who require psychiatric psychotherapy are not suitable—the extremely depressed, those with profound and bizarre disturbances of thought and speech, and those who tend to act out their problems in socially obnoxious and destructive ways. These require a group of their own or referral to a psychiatrist. In the initial interview, the counselor also decides which group will minister best to the person and which group his gifts will serve best.

Once the group is constituted, the task of the counselor is to enable the group to become a group. In fact, his primary focus is upon the functioning of the group as a whole. He does not attempt individual counseling in a group situation. His relationship and attention are primarily to the group as a whole and secondarily to the individuals in it. He seeks to enable the group to serve its members.

How does he accomplish this group-oriented goal and task? This task begins at the onset. Members often look to the counselor for answers and solutions to their problems. The counselor may at first give some gratification of this need to depend. However, he redirects their communication to each other, *so that they begin to look to each other as the source of help*. For instance, instead of answering, the counselor re-addresses a member's question to the group.

The group becomes a group as each member is valued and as his contributions are recognized. The third major function of the counselor consists in seeing *that the group hears and recognizes the contributions of each member.* To speak and be ignored is in a way to be nonexistent. The counselor helps make each member present and existent by seeing that the group does not overlook what each contributes.

Next, the counselor maintains group focus upon concrete experience and immediate group relationships. Members will tend to socialize, philosophize, and theologize. They often discuss persons and situations outside the group. Some of this is necessary in the movement from the emotionally peripheral to emotionally central. The counselor calls the group from abstractions to concrete illustrations of problems of living. He also calls for an examination of feelings and thoughts about persons and situations in the group. As long as one can talk about "out of group" concerns, he can avoid the face-to-face relationships in the immediate group situation.

Furthermore, the counselor *sustains group morale.* For example, he asks the group to examine its silence, its anxiety, and its hostile moments. Left to itself, the members may bog down, become discouraged, or be acutely threatened because of unresolved tension.

Finally, the counselor helps to *make meaning* out of group communications which at times seem to members to be obscure or without point. Occasionally, a member will explode, "Tell us what is going on! I'm lost. What does all this mean?" Group communication coheres around central themes. These are the "hurricane's eye" around which emotional and intellectual turbulence swirls. The counselor keeps track of the "eye" of the turbulence. In fact, one might say he searches for and stays in the "eye," from which he can view the interaction and its direction.

To illustrate, the theme of a recent group session was "behavior programming." The group began by resisting the defensive flight into speech by one member. This member, they said, seldom heard or responded to what another said. Rather he seemed always to have an objective to achieve in a relationship. He related only in terms of what he was trying to sell. His behavior was programmed to avoid direct and mutual encounter. Other members, in turn, discussed how they "programmed" situations at home and at work to be in control, to be the strong one ministering to the weak, or to decide ahead how one was going to be or act. The counselor, identifying the theme and its light, helped the group to "focus the situation" so that the picture was properly "exposed" and less "blurred." All the above-discussed actions on the part of the counselor are, therefore, directed toward maximal functioning of the group as a whole.

Some Dangers in Group Counseling

Interactions in a group become critical, volatile, and explosive. The group counselor must be aware of the dangers which grow out of group behavior and out of his leadership. He must also be competent to deal with "critical incidents." These can only be named here, since limits of space prohibit discussion of specific methods of intervention.

Some persons use a group to fulfill needs for *vicarious living*. Instead of taking the risk involved in new ventures, they feed off other people's experiences. To illustrate, a single girl who fears dating may show more than usual curiosity and interest, to the point of peering or prying into the sexual behavior of another group member. Another member may derive pleasure or satisfaction from exhibiting shocking or sordid details of his or her sexual behavior. This transaction, unless dealt with, perpetuates the problem of both members. In addition, the unrestrained need to talk about group experiences to nonmembers leads to a breach of group confidence. This breach of covenant must be examined, for group effectiveness, as we have seen, depends upon trust between members.

Another person may indulge in *self-pity* and *self-recrimination*. This serves the dual need to be punished and to appeal for affection and love. Counseling calls for bankrupting this pattern of self-derogation, not gratifying it.

The counselor must know when to intervene in *hostile encounters.* The experiencing and communication of hostility happen in counseling. Many Christians feel that all expressions of anger and hostility are wrong. They believe that hostility and anger must be excluded from relationships because they seem un-Christian. Such people become guilty and are unable either to experience or acknowledge their negative feelings. Perhaps this comes from a misunderstanding of the nature of love, as well as from the fear of rejection when they show anger. Christian love does not pertain primarily to how one feels about another, but how one acts toward another. *Christian love essentially is to will the best interests, fulfillment, and well-being of another. Anger, therefore, can be an act of love* when it serves to confront and to work through the conflict in a relationship where another's behavior infringes upon the freedom and negates the personhood of his brother.

In counseling, one works through his hostility so that he comes to experience realistically the many-sidedness of the person who was the object of hostility. For example, a member comes to have feelings of love, sympathy, appreciation, as well as anger, toward significant persons. The counselor seeks to be aware when hostility is misplaced and helps the individual to discover its real source and object. He intervenes, therefore, when attacks occur that involve misplaced hostility. He must judge when anger is misplaced, when it is a defense against closeness, and when it is a healthy expression of resistance against exploitation and manipulation.

Closely aligned with the above are those critical incidents which relate to problems of *submission to or defiance of authority.* A person may unhealthily seek identity in one of three ways: over-identification or identity through merger with a strong person; dominance of a weaker individual; or negative identity in which one is defined by what he is against, not what he is for. Submission, dominance, rebellion call for expert attention.

In the next place, *sexual liaisons* and *subgroup formations* develop in a group. The rule that post-group relationships between members be reported to the whole group aids in dealing with these transactions. Subgrouping occurs when two or more members regularly support each other and exclude others from this "inner circle." Subgrouping has the value of providing security, but it can be divisive and resistive—if what the Apostle Paul calls "party spirit" goes on unattended.

The counselor, too, must be aware of the dangers that accompany his interventions. When, what, and how to interpret are crucial questions. Danger lies in interpreting too much too soon, or in allowing a person to "uncover" too much too soon. Failure at these points can precipitate depression and loss of self-regard. Other questions involve when and when not to gratify members' needs. The counselor, too, will face the issues of either dominance of the group or over-identification with the group, in which he uses the group for his own needs. These are a few of the "critical incidents" which develop and bear within them the potential for ill or for good.

Why Counseling Groups in the Church?

Some readers may think, "All this is well and good for people who have problems, but what place does group counseling have in the church?" [2] A simple answer would be: "The church has always engaged in the care of souls as part of its ministry, and group counseling is a new form its ministry takes." This reply is true but it neglects the deeper and more salient ways in which group counseling is integral to the nature and ministry of the church. In the first place, the church is ultimately concerned that men come into a *saving knowledge of and relationship to God through Jesus Christ*. Group counseling provides a means to *prepare the way* for this knowledge and for this relationship. "To know," according to Biblical understanding, does not consist of ideas or knowledge about God. To know God is to be encountered by Him, to be met in the directness and immediacy of fulfilled moments. God is a living God who reveals Himself through events—His actions in our lives and in history. The Bible is a record of some of these events. However, God works still. He acts and speaks through the significant and insignificant events of each man's life.

In the events of a counseling group, God may be known. In the process of group counseling, events happen which are of profound religious significance. Here one faces the *concrete shape of his own sin*. Here one makes *confession* and hears a word of *forgiveness* and *acceptance*. Here one learns to have *faith*—to trust his brethren and to trust himself. Such existential faith and trust is the ground upon which one may respond in trust to the living God. In counseling, *repentance* and *reconciliation* take place. One turns and becomes reunited to the "Thou" from whom he is separated. Here, too, one learns to become *accountable* to another and to be *responsible* for others. In short, one learns to love another for his own sake. These are many of the "living facts" of the faith which many Christians believe but have experienced only in a limited way.

In addition, as one begins to re-experience, re-evaluate, and re-image himself and others, he discovers that he begins to *re-image his concept of God*. Whether in counseling or elsewhere, we are continually called upon to *break up the images graven in our minds* so that we may be grasped anew by the fullness of the reality of the living God. From the human side, hence, we maintain that group counseling as a method is consistent with the Biblical understanding of "the process of how we know God" and "the process of salvation."

This is not to say that group counseling alone is adequate. It is not. The other ministries of the church are necessary, such as the witness to the Word, the formal and informal expression of worship, and the fellowship and service within the Body of Christ. Group counseling, however, is a method which enables the church to become the church—the covenantal, confessional, caring people of God. It also becomes a place where laymen learn to engage in the prophetic and priestly ministry to each other as they hear confession, offer absolution in the name of Christ, and speak the truth in love.

9. Growth in Receptivity

ROBERT M. COX

Intensive training in the power to listen receptively to other people requires a well-conceived and executed program carried on over a substantial period of time. This demand undergirds the course in Receptive Listening offered at Wainwright House, and elsewhere, by the Laymen's Movement. The process and the outcome of several years of experience with the course are reported here by Robert M. Cox, who was until recently Director of Wainwright House and is now Executive Director of the Center for Organizational and Personal Effectiveness, as well as an Associate of National Training Laboratories.

In writing of this group experience * which began at Wainwright House in Rye, New York, commonly known as the Receptive Listening Course, I would confirm a statement of Dr. James V. Clark:

There is reason to believe that the pedagogy of religious experience has advanced far beyond what many religionists are aware of.[1]

The truth of this observation struck me when, as a member of the national staff of a denominational board of education, I was first involved in a "sensitivity training" experience. At the end of two weeks I was elated and bewildered by what had happened to a heterogeneous collection of men and women. We

* Author's note: This chapter could not have been written except for the concern and assistance of over fifty persons who responded to a questionnaire sent out in order to gain personal comments on the course. The writer not only expresses appreciation to each of them, but wishes there was a way of sharing with readers the glorious warmth of spiritual fellowship that overcame him as he read their personal testimonies.

had little in common beyond an affirmation of the Christian faith and, due to denominational and doctrinal differences, the separations between us were more apparent than any common bond. Nevertheless, under the guidance of a team of behavioral scientists, within this short period we became a group with more concern for one another and deeper interpersonal relationships than I had seen in my national exposure to a major denomination.

The comparison with what happens in our churches continues to disturb me. Similar experiences are being offered to leaders of some denominations, but these will be slow in affecting many congregations. This story of an educational group experience is reported as a challenge which is complimentary to the institutional church, not as a substitute for it. It is in their churches that persons should find a relationship which nurtures growth and fosters the type of search so frequently begun by the course.

Within the process of the Receptive Listening Course— which directs attention to self-understanding and self-acceptance as essential requirements for the understanding and acceptance of others—one is reminded of the Great Commandment "Thou shalt love the Lord thy God . . . and thy neighbor as thyself." But there seems to be little of that self-love, or even self-acceptance, which is necessary for loving one's neighbor; and this is no less true among those familiar with the orthodox doctrine of the Church. For this reason, it is exciting to witness what happens to the relationships within a group when members gain new understanding and acceptance of themselves.

The benefits of the course to society are not always immediately apparent. Yet there is evidence of artists who have begun teaching art to mental patients, teachers who had new relationship and fewer discipline problems with their students, persons who have found new courage in community and occupational issues, not to mention the common strengthening and deepening of family relationships. A prominent outgrowth of the course among graduates is their involvement in a life-long spiritual quest. In this they are undergirded by their awareness of the concern of God and support of others who are involved in this search with them. Some find this can be carried on within their church. Others have to look elsewhere.

The Nature of the Course

To suggest the effect which the Receptive Listening Course has upon individual lives is easier than to describe the experience in a meaningful way. Over and over we have tried to do this in literature and in introductory sessions, but with little success. No comment is more predictably heard from participants in final sessions than "Why didn't you tell us the course would be like this? We didn't know what to expect." This experience restrains the writer from attempting more than a description of the components of the course, as it has been offered in recent years at Wainwright House.

A most important factor is the commitment made by each participant to spend six periods of forty-two hours (usually weekends) with the class, in addition to a considerable amount of reading and some writing at home between these sessions.

Before offering a characteristic schedule for a session, a bit needs to be said about the setting and the principles of leadership involved. A conference center which offers an atmosphere of warm hospitality, modest comfort, serious intent, and some isolation offers the best setting. The more attractive and inspirational the setting is, the more satisfactory it seems to be. Ideally each person or couple would have their own room; however, this ideal is yet to be realized. In some instances, persons living nearby have gone home each night for one reason or another, but almost without exception it is recognized that they have lost something other members of the group have experienced.

The course is conducted on principles of leadership drawn primarily from the client-centered therapy, or nondirective counseling methods, identified with Dr. Carl Rogers. Specific books and written materials are required reading, but not with the idea that the content of these is essential. Rather it is because these relate to common experiences which speak to some personal condition and will be the springboard for deep sharing and new insights. A suggested "group discipline" is distributed at the outset, calling attention to the need for each person to be a responsible member of the class. It encourages each person to: 1) share freely when he has something to offer, 2) see that others have equal opportunity to share, 3) allow time for one message to be heard and taken in before piling on another, 4) make sure that he understands what another person has said before responding to it, and 5) try to maintain a sense of Divine Presence in their midst. An effort is made to convey the idea that no one is there with THE message which all must accept but that each has a contribution to make, and each has the right to accept for himself only those ideas which he can relate to his experience.

A Schedule of the First Weekend

Friday

4:00–6:00 P.M.	Meeting of Leaders—Meditation Room
6:30–7:00	Greeting participants, and room assignments
7:00	Dinner
8:15	** Library—Introductions, followed by discussion of *Venture to the Interior*
9:35	Introduction to "The Use of Silence"
9:45	Break
10:00	Meditation—Meditation Room
	Overnight Silence
10:15	Meeting of Leaders—Office

Saturday

7:00 A.M.	Rising Gong
7:45	Meditation
8:00	Breakfast
9:00	Library—Parable of the Pharisees—Matt. 23:13, 23, 25, 28
10:00	Break—Breathing exercises

** "Library" indicates a general session of the group, which at Wainwright House is held in the library.

10:15	Library—Mote and Beam—Matt. 7:3–5
11:15	Work Period
12:30 P.M.	Lunch
1:45–3:45	Creative Period—Art and Writing
3:45	Break
4:00–5:00	Library—Mary and Martha—Luke 10:38–42
5:00–6:00	Horizontal Hour—Quiet is maintained
6:00	Dinner
7:15	Hymn Sing
7:30	Library—Introduction to Analysis Chart
8:30	Break
8:45	Library—Discussion of experience of members which has brought insights into their lives
10:00	Meditation
	Overnight Silence
10:15	Leaders' Meeting

Sunday

7:00 A.M.	Rising Gong
7:45	Meditation
8:00	Breakfast
9:00	Library—Summary and Discussion
10:15	Assignments for Session II
10:35	Explanation of Corporate Worship
10:45	Break
11:00	Corporate Worship
12:30	Dinner and Adjournment—followed by Leaders' Meeting to plan Session II

Comments on the nature of the first weekend will put some flesh on this skeleton. The leadership team usually consists of about three to five persons with an approximate balance between male and female, which is also desirable in the group. Prior to the beginning of each weekend the team will have determined which person is to be "in the chair," or responsible for each activity, including the meditations. Leaders not in the chair assume a supportive role, participating as members of the group, alert to need for clarification but careful not to short-circuit the group process.

Each leader has a manual for the course which offers helpful suggestions for the leadership of each activity. For example, the major discussion on the first evening is based on the book *Venture to the Interior,* by Laurens van der Post, which is to have been read in advance. Guidance in the manual for the leader of this discussion is:

> Ask some opening question such as, "What did you find in this book that has a bearing on your life and thought?" After this, just wait. Do not get anxious, or be afraid to let the silence do its work. Presently someone will speak, and by that time the others will be ready to carry on.

A suggested opening question for the discussion of Bible passages may be: "What is this trying to tell us?"

The above schedule presents as much description of other activities of the weekend as this chapter will allow except for a few words about the "Creative Period" and the "Corporate Worship." During the former period the group is usually divided in half so that some work at creative writing while the others work with such art media as clay, finger paints, pastels, etc. At the end of an hour each moves to the other assignment. Guidance from the leader's manual best explains this activity:

> Certainly learning to paint is not our aim. Neither are we trying to produce works of art in any medium. Whether the resulting piece is a good composition or beautiful, is simply coincidental. One of the efforts in the course is to sense the great capacities there are which lie below the level of consciousness. . . . All our creative energy whether it be put to use in the field of art, business or home-making, or in the subtle search for spiritual growth, comes from the deep psyche. . . .
>
> Another aspect of this activity is that quite often a person gets some really symbolic material into his work, and frequently it nearly bowls him over with the impact of its meaning. . . .

The Corporate Worship is carried on in the manner of the Society of Friends (because it is appropriate to the atmosphere and philosophy underlying this entire experience) and seems least likely to be offensive to the beliefs of persons of any denomination or faith. Each may bring to his silence the richest elements of his own tradition and each may, as moved, bring to the group any prayer, passage, or message that he desires to share. The worship is ended by shaking hands with those within reach, and is followed shortly by the final meal of the weekend.

At Wainwright House and centers where a chapel is available, the group moves to this room for its morning and evening meditation. These usually consist of a brief inspirational reading, a time of silence, and a prayer. Appropriate readings from many sources have been made available to leaders, but always with the understanding that they are free, and encouraged, to use anything they may know of which is appropriate.

Among the major materials used on subsequent weekends are: Fairy tales, Zen quotations, an introduction to the nondirective counseling responses as identified by Carl Rogers, *The Experiment in Depth* by P. W. Martin, *Siddhartha* by Herman Hesse, *On Listening to Another* by Douglas Steere, *Bar of Shadow* by Laurens van der Post, and excerpts from *The Art of Loving* by Eric Fromm, along with numerous other bits of literature. Of these, the one receiving most attention and time is Martin's *Experiment in Depth.*

Largely through the use of these materials, the course is divided rather clearly into two parts. During the first three weekends attention focuses primarily upon increased self-understanding and acceptance, drawing heavily on responses to the depth psychology presented in Martin's *Experiment in Depth.* In the last three weekends more attention is given to understanding others and to ways of establishing a helping relationship with them. The techniques of nondirective counseling are studied and raised to another level through Douglas Steere's *On Listening to Another* and other writings, and group discussion.

Out of a sense of responsibility for the manner in which the course is conducted, the Receptive Listening Committee has established a firm policy that the manual shall not be given to anyone, regardless of personal background, who has not taken the course and been approved, by the committee, as a leader. Recently a foundation indicated interest in publishing the leader's manual in order that it might be distributed generally. In spite of the Receptive Listening Committee's desire to see the course offered in as many places as possible, and their knowledge that ultimately the use of the course could not, and should not, be controlled by them, it was agreed after careful consideration that the selection and training of suitable leaders was more crucial than the advantages which might accrue to Wainwright House through such distribution.

Committed Lay Leadership

In this day when so much is being said of the role of the laity in the world—and yet such small roles are being given to them in many of our churches—it is noteworthy that all the leadership for these courses, now offered in over six locations, is given by laymen. Frequently they have traveled considerable distance to make this possible. One course required one couple to fly over 1,800 miles on each of the six weekends, while the other couple of the leadership team drove about 250 miles. Although only a small proportion of people are sufficiently sensitive, secure, and trusting for the leadership role which is required, it has been possible to identify among the graduates those who are, and to prepare them through an apprentice role. This has provided a reservoir of leaders for the courses at Wainwright House as well as elsewhere.

Leaders must be men and women who are able to raise important questions for members of the group and then sit by confident that the most satisfactory answers for each person will be those which he finds related to his own experience. They must have confidence that the design and content of the course will touch each person at a deep level if the leaders "stay out of the way" and give it time. They must be sensitive to the feelings of those in the group and know when and how to raise a question that may turn attention from one person or help the group move to a deeper level. But they must also be ready to share from their own experience when it can foster interdependence within the group rather than dependence upon the leader. Because of the freedom and openness within the course and the unique nature of each group, almost every leader has commented on the degree to which he has grown and gained new insight from each experience, and a new appreciation for the special quality of each class. But even these are small rewards compared to one's observations of the course's effect upon most of those who take it.

A Process of Development

Space does not allow adequate comment on the dynamics of this group experience. However, attention is called to one common characteristic in this course, sensitivity training and some other "encounter" groups. A group goes through three stages of behavior: Dependence, Counterdependence, and Interdependence. These are given substantial attention in the literature about "sensitivity training" or "T-groups." Most of us go to a new group expecting to find the authority in a fairly strong leader. When this is not evident, we are likely to express varying degrees of dependence by appearing confused or helpless and looking to the leader to move us on. If the leader of the group fails to respond to this appeal as we desire, we tend to challenge him and his leadership or to reject him. Here one sees expressions of counterdependence. In the process of these expressions, group members will usually resolve their concern or anxiety about the leader and begin to accept mutual responsibility for what happens in the group. Beyond this they find a sense of solidarity and establish a standard for their level of exchange, which makes possible the interdependence through which groups are most helpful to their members.

It is usually apparent in the initial stages of this course that most of the participants would prefer a more directive type of leadership. Unlike the sensitivity group where the counterdependence is very likely to be expressed by direct challenges, struggles with and rejection of the "trainer," here it is more likely to come out in expressions of dissatisfaction or anger related to materials, methods, or thoughts of the one in the chair. In the manual, leaders are warned of this group phenomenon and encouraged not to "fight back" or become defensive when thus challenged. Consequently, by the third or fourth weekend an interdependence is usually apparent which allows the group to develop a high degree of trust and to enjoy sharing ideas and concerns which are of utmost personal importance but seldom discussed in society. That this occurs without the more dramatic, and sometimes traumatic, personal upheaval of some group experiences seems commendable for the sake of most persons involved in this course.

The greatest impact of the course comes to each participant as a result of the unusual relationship which he experiences within the group. Reactions at the end of the course consistently reflect appreciation for the level of the relationship. Although attention is given to "techniques" of helpful listening, the participants discover that they have learned "to listen to each other with our hearts" and to love each other "because we understand." As a result, many of the groups continue to meet on a periodic basis, and one has met monthly for over nine years. But herein may lie a basic question. Do we mistake the relationships in this group for individually internalized change in relationship with others? Is the acceptance realized here projected beyond its real effect? Can these people really listen with empathy and understanding to others with whom they must relate outside the course sessions?

On occasion there has been reluctance on the part of the leaders to include in a class those who may be less readily acceptable. The question has arisen whether the course is really open to many who are not among the more affluent, with time and money for indulging in such self-fulfilling pursuits. While taking some delight, verging on pride, in our "acceptance," it is in reality limited to those who, being like ourselves, are easy to accept and understand. There is in this warm glow the common danger of hypocrisy.

For the author there is a further question which would require research for its answer. Does this tendency toward homogeneity within the groups, the resultant limited conflict to be dealt with, and the literary material studied have a limiting effect on the depth of the "leveling" which takes place and the ultimate acceptance? Other group experiences in which the focus is on "here and now" aspects of their life together may be more likely to encounter conflicts which severely test the acceptance level in the group. Consequently, members of such groups may arrive at deeper understanding and increased ability to accept what previously would be unacceptable.

Testimonies to the impact which the course and the accompanying group relationship have had upon individual lives vary from one person to another. Frequently it is the story of a man who has made a significant vocational adjustment out of discovery that he is not doing what he most wants to do with his life, or out of a new-found courage and support for making a change which he has not previously dared to make. Among these are the electrical engineer who, with a family of five children and having just completed a new house which he and his wife had practically built with their own hands, left his job, sold his home, moved to a university community, and began work on a doctoral degree in educational psychology. He writes now that he is "doing much more interesting work. Perhaps more important, my family life is many times more rewarding." We continue to learn of persons for whom this experience has had vocational significance, but it is most frequently spoken of for the effect which it has had upon their personal growth and effectiveness, or spiritual insights and understanding. For one man it was his participation in the course which he credits with lifting him above the "humdrum monotony of life, job and vocation and awakening him to an inner creativity that has overcome anxieties regarding any future job change or retirement."

Repeatedly we are told of the degree to which this experience has enabled persons to move beyond religious truths as intellectualized knowledge. One significant testimony is that of a grandmother who has told of the manner in which her "strong core of the old Puritanical" had caused her to live a life of dutiful service and then more service. However, through the course she became convinced that "an all-loving God cares for me as much as those whom I serve. . . . I am no longer motivated by 'doing good' but can relax and let good work through me. I have gained a much deeper companionship with God. . . . We are doing things, quietly and gently together." There is no doubt in the minds of those who have worked with this course that man's religious experience is enhanced by an open search which takes into account his psychological nature and the contributions to be found in other segments of his heritage. Beyond this it has been seen that rather than separate men from their religious traditions it deepens their appreciation of them. However, it may also sharpen their criticism of that within the church which is unworthy of its basic nature and purpose. It places at the center of one's life the search for the Kingdom of God.

10. Professional Interpersonal Groups

CONRAD SOMMER

> The arena in which interpersonal groups function is often
> seen as being the local congregation. But their possible use-
> fulness in other areas is now being rapidly expanded. This
> chapter, and the one following, offer two significant examples.
> Dr. Conrad Sommer describes the results of a group process
> in which professional practitioners have engaged under his
> leadership, and the methodology used to bring about these
> results. He is Past President and Past Medical Director of the
> Psychoanalytical Foundation, of St. Louis, and lectures at
> Eden Theological Seminary, as well as being engaged in
> private psychoanalytical practice.

This chapter describes some experiences—not in the church—
with helping professionals in small groups, that confirm the
value of groups for teaching and for professional and personal
development. Experience with (1) a preformed group, (2) a
graduate class of ministers in a seminary, and (3) a group that
had to be formed, is described. This last group, of medical doctors drawn from a half dozen medical specialties, will be
described first and in greatest detail.

The "Balint" Technique

The work with the medical group was inspired by and mod-
eled after Michael Balint's work in London, as described in his
book *The Doctor, His Patient, and the Illness*.[1] Dr. Balint
formed groups of some twelve general practitioners, who took
turns in presenting to the group, with Dr. Balint or one of his
colleagues present, their most difficult current problem-patient

situation. One must add "situation" to "problem-patient," because it is often not the patient so much as perhaps (1) the patient's family, (2) the doctor himself, (3) other medical specialists to whom the patient may have been sent, or other elements in the situation that cause the troubles. As these doctors took their turns in presenting their vexatious and anxious patients (and selves), a small but very gratifying personality change quite regularly occurred in them. Some details of both the problems encountered and the personality growth in the physician will be given from our St. Louis experience.

Forming a Balint Group

I purchased two dozen copies of Dr. Balint's book and mailed them with a covering letter to a list of fifty physicians whose names had been suggested to me as being interested in the emotional problems of their patients. One or two of the fifty were angry (one threatened to throw Balint's book away if I did not pick it up promptly), but an interested group of fourteen was formed, held a luncheon meeting, and picked an evening for a fortnightly 90-minute session with a commitment for at least one year's experience. We had made it a requirement that no one should be admitted to the group unless he had read the Balint book and would make a commitment of regular attendance for a substantial period of months.

The original group comprised six internists, three pediatricians, three gynecologists, one urologist, and one psychoanalyst (myself). During the first two and one-half years of this group's experience (45 sessions), there was a small turnover with physicians from other specialties also participating: dermatology, orthopedic surgery.

Heterogeneity in the Group

At the outset, we had one major difference from Dr. Balint's groups, whose participants had the common denominator of all being general practitioners. We also had sharp differences in the degree of psychological sophistication in the members of the group. Three of the men had been psychoanalyzed some years previously, and were seasoned and leading practitioners in their three respective specialties. They were quite willing to have quite inexperienced and psychologically naïve physicians join them in this learning experience. Their spirit introduces the next topic to be discussed.

The Unifying, Homogenous Element in a Balint Group

This element could be called a brotherly sharing in the task of overcoming trouble, i.e., anxiety, guilt, shame, inexperience, and defensiveness in the physician, and similar tensions in patients and relatives. Each physician soon learned that every member of the group had tensions comparable to those he suffered, that each one welcomed the help of the group, and that the urgent need of the presenting physician stirred both a deep wish to help in the others present and a suddenly increased capacity to do so. In that urgent, nascent situation, the presenter also often experienced a breakthrough of self-understanding, and of understanding of the patient. We had, then, a dozen men who were able to be genuinely concerned, generously listening participants in the solving of the doctor's problem, his patient's problem, and the problems in the doctor-patient-family, etc., relationships. In this mutuality there is a strong unifying group homogeneity.

Method of Presentation

As already stated, it was mandatory that the patient situation presented fulfill three requirements:

1. The situation was failing and the presenter strongly needed and wanted help.
2. The situation was current, and alive, the patient still coming to the perplexed physician for help.
3. There were misunderstood, baffling, and/or possible unknown or unsuspected emotional factors in the patient or in the doctor, that might be clarified in the group.

The presentation was *not to be read, nor written out,* in advance. The medical record and jotted notes could be brought and referred to, but not presented as a reading. This method of presentation elicits the physician's feelings about the patient, about himself, and about the doctor-patient relationship.

There is a sharp contrast between typical medical records consisting of externally oriented factual items and the alive, unread oral report, wherein the presenting doctor suddenly realizes how he has really felt about the patient situation. The intention and the opportunity (in the presence of understanding colleague-brothers) to put outside himself, in clarifying words, that which had been unclear inside him like an amorphous, opaque jelly feeling, does indeed bring clarification, relief, and confidence. I cannot emphasize too strongly the value of the unread, spontaneous method of presentation. Interest, not boredom, is elicited.

The listeners were permitted to break in at any point with questions, comments, and often sympathy or laughter. We had frequently to check our inclinations to interrupt, lest we interfere too readily with our colleagues' presentation.

Problems and Situations Presented

At the end of the first year, I examined some of the typical records made from our taped seminars and gave each a title. Most were single patient presentations, some a general problem in which data from several patients was presented. Some of the latter titles are:

"Impotence"—by a urologist
"Enuresis"—by a pediatrician
"Difficult Parents"—by a pediatrician
"Sterility"—by a gynecologist.

Some of the more specific individual cases were titled:

"A 15-Year Treatment"—by an internist
"Multiple Symptoms in a Dependent Woman"—by a gynecologist
"A Case of Chronic Pelvic and Psychic Pain"—by a gynecologist
"A Case of 'Dependent' Hysteria"—by an internist
"Possible Early Paranoia"—by an internist
"Years of Scratching and Infecting the Face"—by a dermatologist
"Suicide Danger"—by an internist

"An Irritating Patient"—by an internist
"Many Accidents and Mishappenings"—by an internist.

Growth or Changes in the Doctors

Inferences of helpful changes in the doctors' attitudes and capacities may be drawn from some of their remarks in the later seminars.

A pediatrician: "This is the kind of case I could not have handled before because I was too intolerant of the mother's rejection of the child."

An internist during his third presentation: "I made five mistakes in trying to work with this man." However, the group was able to tell the presenter that his enlarged capacity to recognize his errors, and the ability nevertheless to continue to work with the patient demonstrated the changes in him over his earlier presentations.

Gynecologist: "I no longer rise and fall as much with the patient's rise and fall in mood or anxiety."

Several physicians: "I understood my over-anxiousness and irritability with difficult patients better. I can think about them, instead of blindly reacting to them and either doing too much or too little, or the wrong thing."

The individual presenter tends to be self-critical, doubting his feelings, his motivation, his judgment, and the effects of his efforts upon the patient. The group has much more distance between itself and the patient, and hence, much better perspective. Thus, the group's judgment upon the presenter is usually much less harsh than his own upon himself, a factor of considerable importance in the development of needed confidence.

Thus, confidence in one's own intuition, the courage to act on it, and perhaps a more "active" intuition may be the principal growths that occur. The opened perspective on the unconscious elements operating in patient and physician provide the latter with almost unlimited material for the consideration of his activated intuition.

That such freeing of physicians may lead to their undertaking too difficult treatment tasks is a fear that is justifiable in the case of the careless physician. The conscientiousness of the members of our St. Louis group prevented such unwary, careless adventuring, a possibility which requires continuing watchfulness.

Occasionally, a physician had no insight of how poorly he had handled a patient situation. Can he be criticized clearly enough in the benign atmosphere I portray? Are such mistakes confronted or swept under the rug? In an open group, such a blind error-maker usually does not fit in or stay, unless he can readily be helped to see. If the group thinks he can learn, someone will call attention to the egregious error just described, but not recognized, by relating a similar "error-with-blindness" from his own experience. Usually confrontation does occur: "That was a very bad thing you did!" Evasion of the confrontation would certainly undermine the group's confidence that the members would deal in full honesty with each other.

A Preformed Seminary Graduate Group

A similar approach and technique has been found to work well with experienced clergymen taking part-time graduate training while continuing in their pastorates in congregations or specialized chaplain ministries. To date, three classes ranging in size from eight to twelve members have been worked with. Two professors of theology and a psychoanalyst were regularly present at each weekly two-hour session (3 quarters, 33 sessions). The first hour of each session was spent in a discussion of assigned readings, the second hour was spent in a "case" presentation. Years spent in the ministry ranged from one to twenty-five, with a mean of seven and one-half years. Fifteen per cent were in general pastorates, chiefly "one-pastor" churches.

This was the first course in a master's curriculum in pastoral care, ambitiously entitled: "The nature of man." The readings were theological-philosophical (Tillich, Kierkegaard, Niehbuhr, etc.) and psychological-psychoanalytic (Freud, Erikson, etc.). Thus, the subject matter went beyond personal counseling. We opposed any tendency on the part of the occasional chaplain who, in presenting his own case, wished to "instruct" his admittedly less-experienced-in-counseling pastor colleagues, instead of seeking *their* help.

The pastors differed from the physicians in having had less ongoing individual responsibility for most of their parishioners. They rarely had written records, certainly not in detail (except some chaplains). Like Balint's general practitioners, however, they had some long-time knowledge of families and individuals in the church, which was of considerable value in judging the potentials of acute situations brought in for counseling—or, not brought in, but threateningly hanging over the pastor. The following list illustrates some of the problems the pastors brought for help from their fellow students and from the faculty:

Numerous instances of marital discord,
of alcoholism,
of parental-adolescent discord,
of chronic psychosomatic health problems,
of adolescent upheavals, identity crises,
of breakdowns and chronic character problems in adults.

Also there were: grief situations, premarital counseling, the journey to Selma, Alabama, with a score of university students, prayer with the football team, friction with the senior pastor, inability to deal with the church scandal-monger, "do I belong in the ministry?", etc.

Example: Praying with the Football Team

I felt acute embarrassment when a campus chaplain member (J.E.) of our first seminary class announced his case presentation as being his anxiety about praying with the university football team immediately before and after each game. My prejudgment was that this would surely be a misplaced taking of the sacred into the secular. However, we who began with scorn "remained to pray." J.E.'s serious work with the football team had won the confidence of the players. Several of them were now coming to this campus minister with their personal problems. The position of kneeling on *one* knee—being both the position of the football line and the praying football player —and the intensity of feeling of the lineman in anticipation of his own charge and that of his opponent matching the intensity of genuine prayer were among the "ingredients" J.E. used so well with the players. The prayer was not for victory, but for the best playing, the honest playing, for freedom from crippling injury on either team, etc.

Possibly, this example sounds too much like a report on a success. However, J.E. was far from sure that what he was doing was right and actually wanted and needed both our questions and our final hearty affirmation. It was a moving learning experience for all of us. Occurring in the early days of this seminar group, it did much to open us up to each other and draw us together into an operative brotherhood.

I presume just as medical schools could (and are beginning to) better prepare their students in the kind of patient responsibility the physician learned to take in our Balint group, so such additional preparation, too, should be and is beginning to be undertaken in the seminaries. Some learning perforce cannot come before one gets his feet well wet in responsible work situations where pressures and responsibilities are greater than in the seminary.

A Seminar of Dentists

I met monthly for a year with a preformed group of practicing dentists, organized as a monthly study group dining club. This quite cohesive group had been in existence for eight years and accepted a year of Balint seminars as an additional self-development learning experience. The men took turns in presenting their emotionally baffling patients with problems such as: The young woman who unnecessarily (from the dental standpoint) wanted all her teeth extracted; patients whose jaw tensions repeatedly interfered with occlusion solutions; or the treatment of dental problems causing pain in the tempero-mandibular joint; fearful patients; suspicious, paranoid, depressive, angry patients and complementary feelings in the dentists. The members of this group were very helpful with each other in becoming more aware of their anger against certain patients, more accepting of the problems involved, and wiser in the handling of the patient's feelings and the doctor's own feelings.

A Seminar Group that Did Not Jell

An effort to develop a seminar among campus ministers from several universities was only minimally successful, the group being disbanded because of poor attendance in the third quarter of its existence. This was not a preformed group. I had not, nor had anyone else, done the rather large amount of preliminary work that had been done in forming our initial physicians' Balint group.

The Role of the Moderator

In emphasizing the brotherly relationships of the members of these groups, I have so far neglected the discussion of my own role. The presenter always sat at the head of the table, I usually sat at his immediate right or left. I was a highly respected authority figure, believed to have superior knowledge, which was, however, sparingly dispensed. I delayed my comments so that the members would be under pressure to exercise their own knowledge and intuition. They knew that if their formulations or advice went too far astray, I would speak up. Also, if there were specific dangers for or in the patient (suicidal or homicidal dangers), I would naturally speak up. In addition, the members would consult me after the group sessions about referring the patient for psychiatric consultations or treatment, if either seemed indicated. One could say that the groups took a certain comfort or security in the fact that they had in me a reliable fund of knowledge that could be drawn on at any time of real necessity, after the members of the group had done their best, not before. They knew I could be relied on to ask additional questions and raise additional pertinent issues. An ideal moderator would perhaps know "everything," but would speak sparingly.

The groups often asked me to give them "little lectures" on psychoanalytic topics such as transference or countertransference. I rarely complied. I did intervene to restore the balance if one or more of the more sophisticated physicians or chaplains began lecturing or "throwing his knowledge around" in a way that confused or intimidated the more naïve members of the groups.

Factors Helping or Hindering the Success of Balint Groups

1. Unformed groups should not be begun without sufficient advance work. Prospective members of such classes must understand well enough what they are getting into that they will sign up with the solid intention of participating regularly for a substantial length of time.

2. Time is needed for people to become open about themselves, and with each other. I suspect that some of the emotional growth that occurs is not at the conscious level. Some of the defensiveness to be overcome may require several penetrations, perhaps spaced months apart, by hearing how others in the group handled problems in the area of special sensitivity for any particular member of the group.

3. Maturity. There must be at least several persons in a given group with a degree of maturity to enable these "core" members to be seriously open about substantial problems with difficult patients, clients, members of the congregation, etc. Beginners in the professions have neither succeeded nor failed enough to be suitable as the *only* members of a Balint group, nor are they likely to be able to commit themselves sufficiently to a Balint undertaking.

4. Thus, a group of seriously neurotic professionals who

need to be in individual psychotherapy would not be a good nucleus for a Balint group. By definition, Balint groups are not group psychotherapy groups; they are training groups, mutual consultation groups from which, however, reports of serendipity experiences happily do come of individual emotional growth.

5. Perhaps, then, only among the most caring and capable of our professional people may we expect the most frequent good Balint experiences to occur. This is certainly a point to be challenged by efforts to organize groups a little lower down in the "caring and capable" scale in the several professions. Our own St. Louis experience showed how well less experienced, somewhat naïve, but strongly conscientious and caring physicians did do in the Balint situation.

6. I would like to inform other psychiatrists and psychoanalysts how gratifying these experiences were to me. Medically, I learned a great deal about what is going on in the other medical specialties. It was valuable, too, to be taken vicariously into the congregations, into the dental offices (painlessly!), and onto the turbulent university campuses. Most of all, it is a rare privilege to be a participant in the growth experience of some of the most capable and devoted members of our helping professions.

Should Professional Interpersonal Groups Be Continuing or Short-Lived?

Does the Balint technique grow stale and run into diminishing returns if extended over several years? My longest experience with a group was two and one-half years, to which another year was added with one of my esteemed colleagues replacing me as moderator. Although there certainly are individuals who are always "learning without learning anything," there are also gifted and caring professional people who resume growth and are eager for learning situations over several decades of professional life. They bring balance, wisdom, leadership, and "goodness" to their professional groups and should secure for themselves additional group learning opportunities from time to time.

Does this chapter belong in a "religious" book? Yes, if one regards as "religious" the feeling and practice of brotherly helping, the reduction of guilt, ignorance, and timidity, and the increase of venturing, of confidence, and of competence in the service of those who come to us for help.

11. Parish Occupational Groups

ROBERT BATCHELDER

JAMES CAMPBELL

Earliest and most significant of the attempts to bring the church into relation with the industrial order, the Detroit Industrial Mission has accumulated a large body of experience and insight into the ethical problems confronting lay people engaged at all levels in the industrial enterprise. In this chapter, that experience is described in terms of occupational groups created in the parish to deal with the problems men face in their daily work. Dr. Batchelder, formerly of the D.I.M. staff, is now Associate Professor of Christian and Social Ethics, and Director of the Center for Urban Ethics, at the Hartford Seminary Foundation; and James Campbell recently succeeded Hugh White as Executive Director of the D.I.M.

"I just don't look at the church as an instrument for providing help in organizing or running my life."

"A person almost has to be a Dr. Jekyll and Mr. Hyde to relate faith and work."

So spoke a top manager and a production worker—both active churchmen. These statements express a truth for most nominal Christians, not to say people outside the church. Very little connection exists between Christianity as it is taught and understood within church life and the issues men find themselves up against in the midst of their work in today's business and industry.

The Detroit Industrial Mission seeks to stimulate discussion of significant issues with individuals and with groups of men at various levels in industry—in management offices, on the assembly line, in the engineering laboratories, at the union hall, in the executive dining room. Discussions focus on issues and problems of central importance in that particular place of work. D.I.M.'s purpose is to stimulate men to look beneath the surface at the human and ethical dimensions of these issues—and to encourage men to move from fresh insight to constructive action within the area of their responsibilities.

Basically the style of D.I.M. is one of give-and-take rather than preaching. Meetings take place in industrial plants and offices more often than in church buildings. Conversations center on men's responsibilities in such areas as production, efficiency, collective bargaining, technological improvements —rather than on traditional "churchly" or "religious" topics.

Parish Occupational Groups

In its eleven-year history, in addition to devoting its major effort to direct work with men in industry and labor, D.I.M. has tried various ways of relating to local congregations. Gradually the "parish occupational group" evolved as one simple but effective method whereby the questions of faith and work could be fruitfully attacked within the local parish setting.

In essence, a parish occupational group consists of fifteen or twenty men recruited from one large church or from several neighboring churches, all of whom work in the same type of job, such as salesmen, engineers, production workers, or managers. The group meets for a series of five or six weekly sessions and then concludes. The purpose is to provide a format in which men can freely and frankly explore the relation between their religious faith and the important issues of their work— and thereby strengthen these men for carrying out their primary ministry as Christians at the place of their responsibility in the secular world.

How does a group like this get started? What happens at its meetings? What impact or results do they produce? Let us answer these questions in order.

Getting Started

The first decision to be made is whether to draw the group from a single church or from several neighboring churches. The typical parish church has men from a variety of vocations, but not enough from any single type of occupation to form a parish occupational group. Therefore, we ordinarily draw men from a group of from three to six nearby local congregations.

Since the parish occupational group is designed for laymen and focuses on the issues of their work, it is imperative to have laity involved in the initial planning and recruiting steps. This means that as soon as we have described the concept to the priests or pastors of the churches and enlisted their support, we ask each clergyman to name a strong layman in the target occupation to serve on an organizing committee. We will meet with this committee, go over the whole plan, offer samples of the case studies and other materials that might be used, jointly prepare a recruitment sheet, choose a day of the week and set the time for the meetings, and arrange for other details.

This planning session is a very important moment, because it is the participation and momentum of this committee that will carry the series. We need their understanding, enthusiasm, and leadership. If the lay committee assumes full responsibility for running the group, so much the better—but the pastor must at least be tolerant, and should certainly be kept informed of the group's progress.

Sometimes it is possible to organize a group in a single church, if it has a large congregation with a concentration of men in the same occupation. Again, we work with the pastor and with a committee of laymen. In this case one solidly enthusiastic layman with the pastor's help can make all the difference. Our experience is that as soon as we make known the down-to-earth meaty kind of discussions we're talking about, with sample topics and case studies that deal with real problems of the daily grind, there is little trouble generating enthusiasm.

The advantage of working in only one church is that the series may have relatively greater impact on that total church and its pastor. That is, there's more chance of helping that congregation focus its mission *outward* toward the world. Moreover, the meeting mechanics are easier.

Recruiting a group from several churches, both Protestant and Catholic, has certain real values that are missed if the effort is limited to a single church. The group becomes a grass-roots ecumenical venture at the start. Moreover, the interplay of different religious orientation gives a more varied perspective on the issues that will be discussed.

Recruitment by personal contact is the best method. An engineer calling a fellow engineer and inviting him to join in an examination of their mutual occupation cuts more ice than an announcement in a church bulletin, a request by the pastor, or a mimeographed letter received at home. We have found that personal recruitment can be enhanced by having something definite on paper stating the nature and purpose of the group.

We urge the committee to aim their recruitment particularly at men on the fringe of the church's life, rather than those who are already at the center, serving on three committees, singing in the choir, and teaching Sunday School. Many men feel themselves marginal to the church precisely because they find the center of their life in their work—and they feel the church has had little to say about what is most important to them. The parish occupational group can be a means of involving these men in the life of the church in a way that will mean something significant to them. Men of this type also bring a valuable realism and critical perspective to the discussions.

The committee recruits between twenty and twenty-five men in order to assure a consistent group of from fifteen to eighteen at any one meeting. Attendance will vary according to the time of year, which night of the week the group is meeting on, and the quality of the discussions. Our experience has shown that an absence rate of 25 per cent on a given evening is normal.

We find that two hours is a good length for the meetings. We begin and end on time—a refreshing experience for church members who are used to interminable evening meetings at church!

Finally, it is helpful to designate one person who is responsible to arrange in advance for the mechanical details: writing pads, pencils, a roster of participants listing addresses and places of work, a blackboard or large tablet, chalk or felt-pen markers, name placards that can be seen from one end of the table to the other. The room is arranged so that each man sits at the table and is able to see all the other participants; an arrangement of chairs in rows (so that people look at the backs of heads) is taboo. A pot of hot coffee helps lubricate the conversation—either before the meeting starts or at a midway break.

The Content of the Meetings

Almost the entire first session is spent in introductions. This may sound tedious, but it isn't if it is done right. First, there is a three-minute statement by the chairman, an articulate lay member of the committee. He calls the meeting to order, welcomes the members, and briefly states the nature and purpose of the whole series:

> We are going to focus on issues in the area of our ordinary jobs, not issues internal to the church.
>
> We want to probe these issues from the perspective of our Christian faith.
>
> The process will be one of learning from and sharing with each other in informal discussion and frank expression of opinion.

Next comes a statement by the D.I.M. staff member, explaining what Detroit Industrial Mission is and why it is involved in meetings like this. He then continues with a concise summary statement about the ministry of the laity: the ministry of the church takes place primarily in the world, not in the church building . . . it is carried out primarily by the laity, not by the clergy . . . it is concerned with truth, wholeness, reconciliation, and justice in the places where Christians already

bear secular responsibility. The purpose of these meetings is
to put flesh and blood on this concept, specifically in terms of
the particular occupation in which the members of the group
make their living.

These preliminaries out of the way, we then proceed around
the table to have each man introduce himself *vocationally*
(*not* how many children he has, or what responsibilities he
holds within the church). Where do you work? What are your
responsibilities? What kinds of decisions do you make? What is
your relationship to your superiors and to your subordinates?
What are your main problems and satisfactions in your work?

Men are encouraged to question one another as the introductions proceed. The point is to get as full a picture as we can
of each man's job situation—and still get around to everyone
before the evening is over.

It is amazing how men who have known each other for years
in church activities can actually know so little about what they
do during working hours. This process of self-introduction contains a dimension of discovery that always proves fascinating
and prevents the group from becoming bored. Men get acquainted with their friends at a new and deeper level. The
pastor suddenly learns aspects of his men's lives that he has
never had the opportunity or interest to discover before.

At least fifteen minutes is saved at the end of the meeting
for two final items. First, in bringing the introductions to a
close, the point is made that *what the group has just described
is the arena of their ministry*. It is precisely in the midst of the
ordinary duties and problems they have been talking about
that they have the opportunity and responsibility to serve their
fellow men: this is their personal part of the church's total
mission.

Then the leader asks each man to write out on a sheet of
paper two recurring unresolved issues he faces in his work. An
"issue" can be defined as "that point where two conflicting
human drives collide," or simply a point of human or ethical
conflict. It is good to give one example, such as: "The division
manager continually by-passes my boss to give orders to me."

Or, "There's increasing cynicism in my shop because the management talks quality—but when the chips are down, quality is always sacrificed to production."

It is best to have each man write out his own issues, not only in order to have a complete record, but to be sure we get everyone's thoughts. If we were to ask each man to state his issues verbally, we would find some men think: "My issues are not as important as John's, so I'll just second what he said." The leader collects what has been written. If there is still time remaining, some verbal elaboration and exploration of the written issues can be solicited, especially for the more complex ones. Usually that's all there is time for.

The first evening concludes with this point: "In our introductions we described the *arenas* of our ministry. In listing the human and ethical issues we have identified the *raw material* of our ministry. Before next week you will all receive a list of these issues. We will spend the first hour of the next session evaluating the list and picking out the three or four that are most important and common to us all. Meanwhile, the committee will have picked out one issue in advance that we will tackle in the second hour with the aid of a case study. The three or four key issues identified by the group will become the agenda for our remaining meetings."

Following is a list of issues that one group of salesmen came up with:

1. How to deal with the "color barrier" in an office which is completely segregated at the present time.
2. Lack of clear communication of questions and problems in the everyday course of business.
3. Buyers demanding discounts despite the existence of a price list.
4. Lack of empathy by officials of manufacturing plants toward salesmen.
5. How to effectively use my time:
   a. with customer with great potential, demanding much much time and high risk;

      b. with smaller companies, with lower dollar potential, but
      less aggravation and more selling.
6. Whether to increase sales force or remain a "loner."
7. Hiring and training well-qualified men for sales positions.
8. Need to spend more time at home versus pressures of the work.
9. Uncertainty of defense economy; who to do business with.
10. How to hold key employees.
11. Coping with buyer methods.
12. Transfers: pressure to move versus desire to stay put during
    main years of children's education.
13. The overwhelming control by the corporation over the lives
    and movements of administrative sales or executive personnel.

In presenting such issues for exploration we have found it
valuable to embody the issue in a case study that illustrates
the issue in a vivid way, and "opens up" the issue so that men
can immediately get their teeth into it. We count on members
of the group to frame the case studies, drawing upon their own
experience. Here is a typical case written by a sales manager:

The A.B.C. Corporation, a large manufacturer of computers for
sophisticated program application, has an urgent need for young
electrical engineers in field sales. Word has been passed down to
the personnel department, and a large recruitment program has
been initiated in major cities across the country. The basic job
requirements are a degree in electrical engineering and some sales
experience.

William Adams, a twenty-five year old Negro, holds a degree in
electrical engineering from George Washington University, Washington, D.C., and has worked for the three years since graduation
as a salesman for a distributor of new and used business machines.
His calls are made on all types and sizes of firms in the predominantly Negro areas of Washington where business ownership is
mostly Negro. Adams recognized early that the sale of computer
systems was an important growing field and had completed two
years of night school in their study. He hoped this would prepare
him for a better job in this field. When the A.B.C. Corporation ad
appeared in the Washington papers he recognized the opportunity
and telephoned for an interview. Upon learning that Adams had
the qualifications, the A.B.C. representative granted an interview
for the following day.

Following the interview, Adams was told he would be notified in a short time how the company had acted on his application. The plan was to have applicants screened by a district sales manager at a second interview; if accepted they would be sent to A.B.C.'s New York headquarters for three months of training, followed by assignment to a district sales office.

Following the interview, the A.B.C. representative called the personnel manager in New York to tell him of this Negro applicant, and asked what he should do further with Adams' application. Since a Negro had never been employed in A.B.C.'s sales department, nor had ever applied for employment, the personnel manager recognized that a decision by management was necessary. Therefore, a meeting was called including A.B.C.'s vice-president of personnel, vice-president of sales and an assistant vice-president from the executive department.

QUESTIONS:

Assume you are the vice-president of sales. What are the problems as you see them?

What are the short-range and long-range consequences of the courses of action open to you?

What would you do?

The role of the D.I.M. staff person has varied, depending upon the leadership and resources available in the group. Usually he performs at least these tasks: he keeps notes of meetings, prepares and mails one-page summaries after each session, helps an assigned leader prepare for the meeting, helps write up cases or gather other material related to a particular issue. On rare occasions he may lead all the discussions, or supply all the cases. But involvement of members of the group is preferable in sharing discussions and preparing case studies.

As the series progresses, a key role for the leader, whether a D.I.M. staff person or someone else, is to press the issue home. That is, he must not let participants get away with vague generalities or unchallenged clichés; he must keep the discussion from wandering off on unprofitable tangents.

The final evening of the series deals with a particular issue raised by the group—but we have found that it is important to reserve the last forty-five minutes of the final evening for a period of evaluation in which we look back at the series as a whole. What important issues were raised but left unresolved? Where did we achieve a real consensus that can become the basis for action where we work? What new insights did we gain about the nature of our jobs, and the way we operate in them? At what points did the relation of Christian ethics to our work come through clearly? What were the values—and the limitations—of these discussions? With a final summary statement by the D.I.M. staff man or a lay leader, the parish occupational group comes to an end.

Impact

The ultimate goal of a parish occupational group is action. If an issue is real and urgent to the group and we have explored most of the angles to it—well, what are we going to do about it? This question is most fitting when, inspired by the hypothetical case study under discussion, a participant says: "Well, in my situation the issue looks like this . . ." and he goes on to describe what he is facing. Perhaps out of the discussion a course of action for him becomes clear. At the next week's meeting the person is asked, "Did you try it?" And, "How did it work out? In other words, the group is not just looking for assorted new *ideas* about the issues of their occupation; the group becomes a source of encouragement for them to *do* something about those issues—to take action.

What is action? Action is the starting of something new, by word or deed, within the web of human relationships in which we're involved.[1] The whole focus of a parish occupational group is upon this web of human relationships in a particular occupation. We suspect that what the Christian faith can contribute most to our daily lives is: (1) the faith and the hope that starting something new in this web is both possible and worth the risk; and (2) some clues as to what the content or direction of our action might be. The parish occupational group can be a vehicle of both these contributions, as men bring commonly hammered-out values to bear upon real situations.

One limitation of the parish occupational group is its brevity. In a series of five or six sessions, many real issues can be raised, and a consensus approached on how to resolve a few of them. Inevitably, however, many issues are left dangling and unresolved. Should the series be extended so that subjects can be dealt with in greater depth, and unresolved issues tackled?

D.I.M. has steered away from prolonging parish occupational group series. One reason is to avoid spending all its time meeting with men in churches—when its primary commitment is to direct engagement with men inside the institutions of industry. D.I.M. sees its role with parishes as catalytic: planting the seed of an idea which the parishes should assume responsibility for carrying further if it seems valuable to do so.

Frequently men say at the conclusion of a parish occupational group, however, that it has been a rewarding experience and that the series ought to be extended. There is no reason why the series cannot be continued under the leadership of men from the group, with the encouragement and participation of clergy from the congregations involved. However, experience strongly suggests that it is best not to extend the group indefinitely into the future: attendance will begin to drop off and—like an old soldier—the group will slowly fade away. Rather, the series should be extended by mutual agreement for a definite number of sessions to deal with certain specified topics, and then terminated—only to be extended again for another limited span if the group, after conscious evaluation, decides it will be fruitful.

Where does the parish occupational group lead? Besides leading to action on the part of individuals, it ought to lead to further significant thought and discussion—within the context of the job itself. At the conclusion of a series of discussions with engineers, for example, two engineers in a major auto company said to the D.I.M. staff, "There are men we work with in our engineering department who would appreciate exploring some of the things we've been talking about in this series. Will you work with us to set up a series in the engineering building of our corporation?" When these two men approached their colleagues about having a series of discussions in their building at the end of the work day, fourteen out of the first sixteen approached signed up. And this series—held with the approval of management—led to a second one in the same division a few months later. When the discussion takes place within the work context, among men who work with each other daily, the issues become more pointed—and both the possibility and the risk of action become heightened.

In another direction, the church may go on to explore the dimensions of additional vocational areas: medicine, teaching, law, management, or government. And at a further level, D.I.M. has found that it can be exciting to bring together around the same table men from conflicting groups. That is, after a group of production workers have discussed their problems (many of which center on their relation to their foreman) and a group of foremen have explored theirs (many of which involve the problems of supervising workers), we convene a new parish occupational group composed of foremen *and* workers. At this level we try to resolve some of the differences that divide the two groups. The same sort of conflict group—perhaps it should better be called a reconciliation group—can be organized with salesmen and purchasing agents, teachers and educational administrators, union officials and managers.

The results of these groups are unpredictable, but when men in a church membership begin to get the idea that the basic mission of the church is directed *outward* toward the world where they bear responsibility, the impact upon the total life of a local church can be significant.

The Role of the Pastor

What is the pastor's role in a successful parish occupational group? First, the pastor must understand and appreciate the purpose of the group and give it his support. He can back his laymen in the recruiting stage. The pastor is the "manager" of the local church, and he can kill the possibility of a fruitful parish occupational group by apathy or by throwing cold water on the idea.

One or two pastors can profitably attend the discussion meetings, but the pastor's primary role is to keep his mouth shut—at least at the beginning! He must strenuously resist the temptation to "make a theological point" the first time there is an awkward pause in the discussion. The clergyman must lean over backwards to disprove the expectation of the laymen that this is a meeting like all the other church meetings where the pastor does most of the talking.

This silence is not as negative as it seems, for it is a prerequisite for the pastor's role of being an active listener and learner. Being freed to play the role of listener is the most valuable aspect of the parish occupational group for the pastor: here is the opportunity to learn things about the men of his parish— the world they operate in and the issues they struggle with daily—that he has never known before. This knowledge cannot help but enrich his ministry.

Finally—after it has been clearly established that the discussion is being carried by laymen and that it is focused upon their responsibilities in the world, not in a church—the pastor may also assume the role of participant in the conversation. At those appropriate points where he has a contribution to make to the issue being discussed, he may make it—not as *the* answer being handed down from the pulpit, but as a contribution as worthy as any other to be considered, accepted, or modified by the group. Hopefully, his training and insight will enable him to make a genuine contribution without in any way dominating the conversation.

Underlying Assumptions

The theological assumptions which underlie the parish occupational group are essentially those that may be summed up in the phrase "the ministry of the laity." The fundamental assumption is that laymen—the men and women who are the church—are the primary bearers of the mission of the church in our time. They are the line officers and men. They *do* the mission of the church by the kinds of decisions they make and actions they take in the organizations where they work as employees or participate as citizens.

The major function of the clergy and the institutional machinery of the church is to be an aid and resource to the laity in their ministry. There are, of course, times when clergy and the institution take their place in the front line ranks of the church's mission in the world: the civil rights movement is one example. But essentially the proper function of the clergy is to train, stimulate, and encourage the laity to carry out the church's mission in the world.

Unfortunately, we tend to get these roles reversed. Too often laymen are considered second-class citizens in the church, as aides to the clergy—while the prerogatives of management belong to the *full-time* employed staff of the church. The matter should be put the other way around, with the primary thrust of mission specified in terms of work and community responsibilities. It is our conviction that sensitive Christian laymen want to be in on the core mission of the church, not frittering around at the fringes. When they are constantly relegated to the fringes, they become like assembly line workers who feel they aren't really involved in the life of a plant—they become petty, bitter, and even indulge in minor sabotage.

Another assumption embodied in the parish occupational group is that the laity cannot be prepared for mission by listening one by one to the teaching and preaching of the church and then be expected to sally forth as a solitary individual to carry out the church's mission in the world. Preparation for mission must be *corporate and interpersonal*. Men can best be prepared through a process of dialogue, debate, and exploration with others who share the same kind of situation on the job. It is through this process of mutual enlightenment, questions, criticism, and encouragement that new insight emerges and new convictions about what ought to be done can be strengthened.

Parish occupational groups provide one such opportunity for exercising the ethical imagination and for increasing the possibilities of making fitting and obedient choices in daily life. Whether by means of parish occupational groups, or by some other method, this task of relating faith to work must be done if the church is to survive in our day.[2]

12. Listening to Others

Consensus grows that unless members of a group can really hear one another, whatever else they may strive to do sooner or later fails. But listening to one another involves more than an accurate reception of spoken words; it requires a total response of one person to another. Dr. Robert A. Edgar, minister of Central Presbyterian Church in New York City, out of many years' effective ministry through interpersonal groups, has found this growth in our capacity to listen to one another the essential focus for the life and task of the groups he has helped into being; he describes both the process and the outcome of that approach in this chapter.

Prior to coming to Central Presbyterian Church in mid-town Manhattan in 1961, we worked with small groups in a suburb of Chicago. That program, which involved twenty-five couples in "growth groups," is described in *Pastoral Psychology* [1] and in a book by Dr. Russell Becker,[2] a member of the team ministry of that church. Nineteen years of experimentation with these groups, which were structured primarily to help people to listen to each other as persons and not just to their ideas, have resulted in a format found to be most applicable and pertinent here in New York City.

Our present parish, Central Presbyterian Church, is located at 64th and Park Avenue on the north edge of the encroaching business area and the south edge of the high rise apartments. Our appeal has been to the new residents in these high rise apartments and to others across the city who have been hearing about the "Listening Group" program. The first approach is to invite all the people who visit Central once or twice to the

172

manse for an informal evening. This gives new visitors and the pastor and his wife the opportunity to become acquainted in an informal, relaxed atmosphere. The Listening Groups are discussed briefly along with other church programs.

We soon discovered that people who live in the city are basically no different from those who inhabit the suburbs. In fact, the need for opportunities where people may listen in depth to each other is even greater in the city. The complexity of the city with its crowding and pressure breeds even more isolation and loneliness, and the greater consequential need for a trusting and accepting atmosphere. All are aware that no one really listens to another—not even when they are ill or near death. When we share a little about the purpose of the Listening Groups, they usually nod in agreement that few people experience relationships in which they can be truly trusting and honest. This is true even when one is under drugs or while heavily drinking. Much of the energy we could use for self-discovery is being consumed by our efforts to cover up our duplicity.

We speak of how the Listening Groups provide an opportunity to practice the art of listening to others and being listened to as a person. It is a group called together not to study a book, discuss a prearranged subject, or organize to carry out a project. Rather, the Listening Group is designed to help people experience openness and a feeling of acceptance so that members are able to remove part of their masks and to "be themselves" as much as possible.

Since it is difficult to describe the experience in terms or concepts comparable to experiences people have had in other groups, we encourage our new friends to give it a try for three sessions. Then they can decide if this is a group in which they would like to be involved a couple of evenings a month.

We find no difficulty in setting up Listening Groups in city apartments [3] because they are not the typical "house-church," study, or discussion groups. They are not "church"-oriented in the minds of the participants, but "person"-oriented. Usually people are willing to begin with a group as long as they do not think they are being sold religion or some other program the church is trying to promote. Nominal church members respond positively to a Listening Group when they would not go near a Bible study group.

The main difference we have found between the suburb and the city group experience is that groups are more difficult to start and maintain in the city. Although the need is greater in the urban areas and members are always most grateful to be included, the greater loneliness and increased distrust engendered by the city's impersonal character often make them hesitant to begin such an adventure. Also, there is greater mobility in the city. Because of the rapid turnover, we find ourselves constantly adding new members to each group, thereby losing the momentum of rapport and trust necessary for the best acceptance and growth.

How Growth Takes Place

Life-Changing Experiences

Talking a problem out with a group that really listens can alter one's own attitudes. During one session, one man shared his feeling of estrangement from his nineteen-year-old daughter. Group listening made it possible for him to become aware of his responsibility for this estrangement. He discovered that he had not once permitted his daughter to make her own decisions about life—from the clothes she wore to the choice of a college. When he became aware of this, he was genuinely remorseful. But the group's acceptance of him and its sharing of this disturbing insight provided the climate to change. This listening experience gave him the strength to deal positively with his feelings and concerns.

When two people of sharply differing points of view meet to talk in an accepting atmosphere, they come closer to understanding each other. A case in point is a businessman with strong feelings against labor unions who came up against a union official in his group. When he discovered that another member of the group was an officer of a labor union, he felt he should drop out. He was convinced that he would be constantly irritated and irritating if he remained in the group. But after five sessions, the two men found themselves drawn closely together as persons. They were able to disagree freely about social issues as they genuinely accepted each other's feelings. The group as a whole experienced the meaning of *reconciliation*. They were able later to study it in the New Testament with much better understanding and appreciation.

Members of an interracial listening group experienced insights on several levels. Both the Negroes and the white people were able to plumb the depths of the racial problem. One Negro declared that he was reaching the point where he wondered if he could trust *any* white man. The white members raised similar concerns about the Negroes' motives. Several members admitted ambivalent attitudes and guilt feelings about themselves. These questions and feelings were openly faced. The acceptance which resulted from their honesty brought insight and self-discovery to most members of the group.

Fading and mediocre marriages often take on new life as husband and wife see themselves and each other in a new light. One group member had a domineering husband who caused her to feel as if she were something less than a real person. She felt herself inferior. Much to her surprise, she found that the group listened to her and accepted her ideas and feelings just as much as those of her husband. This evoked insights neither she nor her husband thought were in her. Subsequently, a wholeness in their marriage, never before experienced, was achieved. They found a mature freedom to deal with the dilemma of his dominance and her submission.

Listening Through Differences

Good group dynamics have taught us the necessity of requiring people with strongly differing points of view each to repeat in their own words and to the other's satisfaction what the other is saying *and* feeling. When this is done, the understanding of each other's argument is so much improved that their real differences can be dealt with or accepted much more easily, for it is obvious (but frequently forgotten) that one cannot be marshaling his own arguments if he is required to listen this closely to his opponent's ideas. Often when this is done well, the listener responds: "If that's what you mean, I agree with you." Yet when he still disagrees, he can then speak to the exact point of the disagreement rather than simply oppose irrelevant ideas which were triggered in his own subconscious mind, as half-hearing the speaker. We listeners are often so busy deciding what *we* are going to say that we hear only part of what is being *said*—and little or nothing of what is *felt* by the speaker.

Experiencing Christian Love

We have read in our Bibles and heard from the pulpit the *agape* concept of love expressed in the life and teaching of Jesus Christ, but it is in the act of group members practicing the art of loving others, and at the same time experiencing being loved themselves, that they become responsive to the highest loyalties of the Christian faith. They are experiencing first hand this love and acceptance in the Listening Group. They exclaim, "I never realized this is what the New Testament is talking about." This fellowship becomes the word of God in action for many of them.

We are often asked if the Listening Groups ever become Bible study groups. A group may decide on its own to begin a study of the Bible or a book on theology (two of the groups did this a couple of years ago). However, the group then becomes a "content"-centered group, and the "person"-centered growth in depth is diminished. It is usually best for those stimulated to seek Biblical resources to join a Bible study group which meets regularly for that purpose, and then continue in their Listening Group for as long as they need this type of experience.

Moving Out to Mission

In this day of church renewal, we are constantly reminded that the church's main responsibility is to "equip the saints" for their mission in the world.

How well have these Listening Groups prepared the church members for their servant ministry?

Very few of the twenty-five groups in our suburban church and the ten developed here in New York City have gone out on mission *as a group*. However, the record of individual members is different. It is safe to say that 75 per cent of the group's members have become active in mission individually or joined with others for this purpose. These are the people who respond to the appeals to read to the blind, tutor the retarded children, work for civil rights, civil liberties, and other social concerns. Because they have *experienced* being loved themselves, they frequently respond to Christ's call to his servant ministry more quickly than those who are challenged by the spoken words of a sermon or the written words in a book.

In one group, after discussing the 200,000 children in New York City who are two or three grades behind in reading, two members organized a task force in the church to go into Harlem twice a week to work with the East Harlem Protestant Parish remedial reading program. Another pulled a group of our women together to sponsor a remedial reading program at Central, busing the older children here after school. One man and his wife organized a group to picket City Hall on a racial matter sparked by a discussion a week before.

Central Presbyterian Church has set aside 80 per cent of the time of one of its pastors to do research with a group of laymen on how this church located in the heart of Manhattan can use its resources of plant and endowment most fully for Christ's mission in this city. The key leaders in this effort are all members of Listening Groups.

The church needs to know, however, that many of its members are not emotionally equipped to be sent out on mission. Many are motivated by their own needs and end up thwarting

God's will in their self-service. Most of us need a lot of thinking through and sifting out of our own problems and feelings before we are capable of being used by Christ in the world.

Organization of Groups

To bring a group of people together for practice in listening, there is no need for a set pattern or a systematized program. What is needed is a group of congenial people willing to experiment in human understanding.

Getting Acquainted

Meetings usually rotate in members' homes. The first three are scheduled weekly; thereafter, they meet twice monthly.

For the *first* session, it is suggested that each person take ten or twelve minutes to tell about himself—place of birth, childhood, education, marriage, work or profession, hobbies, etc. The pastor can easily set the pattern on this so others will be free to reminisce. Some may need to be encouraged more than others to share in a sort of a life pilgrimage. Each person finds himself enjoying and sharing memories he hadn't thought about in years. The evening is usually a most revealing experience for everyone.

Difficulties of Listening

By the *second* session, the members are ready to get down to the art of listening. Members of the group are asked to recall how much they remembered about each other from the session of the week before. They are amused and quite interested in what they "heard" and why certain things were screened out by some and not by others.

After this common experience of remembering, we are reminded of the natural difficulties all of us have in communication. Douglas Steere [4] tells us that ". . . in every conversation between two people, there are always at least six people present:

What each person *says* is two;
What each person *meant to say* are two more;
What each person *understood* the other to say are two more."

We begin to realize that everything we say is screened through word-symbols which cannot fully express our ideas or feelings, and also through another's comprehension equipment which is colored by many conscious and subconscious attitudes.

We discover that most of us listen to others in order to *classify* them or to *judge* them. We put them in a frame or category and seal them off. We then respond to the frame and never hear or know the *person*.

We realize that our response to other persons is colored by our many unconscious feelings—our unfaced fears, our evaded decisions, our repressed longings. We listen through our own inner feelings and seldom hear the person speaking.

A common occurrence in many groups is that "they all talk at once." Only one person is allowed to speak at a time. It is obvious that very little listening takes place where talking goes on between two or three in different corners of the room.

Since all of us are aware that few people really listen to us, we do not reveal ourselves in depth. We withhold what we really think, feel, and believe. We do not disclose ourselves as persons because we sense that no one cares enough to listen. This is why so many people never know who they are. One must speak in depth to another who cares enough to listen before one knows himself.

Having been reminded of these deficiencies in listening, the leader then outlines the purpose of the Listening Group as a "laboratory" for practicing the art of *agape* (love) listening. The groups are designed to *experience* listening with openness and acceptance, with care and concern, as the members practice the "I-Thou" relationship of *being* persons to each other.

"Listening Laboratory" Begins

With the *third* session, conditions are ready for the laboratory of listening to begin. There is no set subject for discussion. Topics come from group members. The group is ready to start after two minutes of silence for thinking about a concern or issue, which is shared with the group either verbally or in writing. Within ten or fifteen minutes, the group decides which of the suggested subjects seems to be the most interesting and/or pressing. After a few sessions, the group members become remarkably sensitive to personal concerns and are quick to notice an urgency in someone's voice when he suggests a subject. When a subject has been chosen, sixty to ninety minutes are spent in listening to each other's *inner feelings*, not just to their words and ideas, trying to listen with expectancy so as to evoke the fullest capacity of those attempting to share their concerns.

At the close of the discussion of the subject, the group views itself as if it were from above the "laboratory of listening" with an evaluation scale.[5] Each member marks his estimate of how he accepted and understood others, felt accepted and understood by others, and felt about his self-discovery change during the evening. The results are then discussed for from thirty to forty-five minutes. The most insightful self-discoveries usually occur at this time as the members of the group see how they have been responding to each other. They begin to sense what it means to be real persons in this congenial climate of mutual honesty and acceptance.

It is generally understood that concerns or feelings expressed within the group are not discussed elsewhere. It may take a number of meetings for most of the members to trust the group enough to share real concerns, but confidence grows with openness and acceptance. We have never known anyone to reveal more about himself than he was ready to reveal. None have regretted the sharing of their true feelings.

The group is off and running after the third session, meeting twice a month and following the "laboratory listening" pattern each meeting.

Suggestions for Organizing

First Three Meetings

Full attendance the first three meetings of a group is essential to later success. Since the Listening Group is one that is so difficult to describe, the twelve people need to experience together what takes place in the growing and knowing in these early sessions or they never quite "get with it" later on. This is managed by setting up three dates, a week apart, and then inviting the people to all three. If a person cannot attend one of these evenings, then attempt to get him for another group. It usually takes a list of twenty-five people in the city to end up with twelve who are free on the three dates chosen.

They are told that after these three meetings, the group members will decide for themselves if this kind of meeting or fellowship is for them. If not, then they are free to drop out. Ninety-five per cent of those who attend the first three meetings decide to stay on more or less indefinitely.

Selecting Group Members

Listening Groups need to be composed of twelve fairly emotionally stable people. One disturbed or depressed person causes the others to focus on him, and the group becomes centered on him with little listening to the others taking place. The pastor or a leader in his capacity should select the people for the group on the basis of his evaluation of their general emotional health and "hunch" about making the congenial group. Although these are not therapy groups, much insight and self-discovery does take place for the relatively healthy people. One experiences a genuine concern for his being as a person as he begins to trust the members of the group. He can be honest because he senses the honesty of others. In the accepting experience of removing a part of his mask and revealing some of his true feelings, he begins to discover something of who he really is.

Group members may range from twenty-five to seventy years

as long as they have much in common educationally and culturally.

Groups composed of couples have proved to be the most productive. Many husbands and wives have the rare privilege of not only "hearing" each other for the first time, but of being listened to in depth as the group opens the door to continued listening to each other at home. Most couples say they continue the discussion of "what happened" during the evening way past bedtime. Dozens of couples have witnessed to the enriching of their marriage because of the insights coming from their group. Several marriages have actually been saved. Only on one occasion in hundreds and hundreds of meetings has a marriage been threatened. The discussion that evening triggered a domestic squabble that was about to erupt anyway. This, then, opened the way to provide some much needed counseling which led to a healing situation.

Combining couples with single people also makes a good group, as each has an opportunity for a broader range of shared experience.

Groups confined to only single persons have two limitations: (1) the search for a mate inhibits the freedom to be oneself; (2) the mobility of single people is usually greater so that group continuity is diminished. In New York City, groups of single people last, on the average, about nine months. Since it takes three to five months for most group members to become free enough to trust each other sufficiently to share in depth, gains are limited.

Methods of Choosing a Subject

The role of moderator for each meeting automatically is taken by the host or hostess for the evening. A meeting called for 8:00 P.M. should be brought to order by 8:15 by the moderator calling for two minutes of silence for the members to center down to think about the concern or issue they would like to throw in the hopper for the subject for discussion. Any topic is permitted as long as it is one that is of real interest or deep concern for the person suggesting it.

The moderator may provide paper and pencils for each to write his subject, or the group may decide to go around the circle asking each to give his subject verbally. Whether written or spoken, the group members as a whole may briefly question each other to be sure that the concern or subject is understood. Care should be taken not to begin discussing someone's topic at this time of clarification. It is important for all to have a chance to suggest a subject and then decide democratically which one appeals to the majority.

Suggested topics for one group's discussion were:

"Can a businessman be Christian and still succeed?"
"Should the church meddle in politics?"
"What does it mean to be a Christian in our day?"
"What is man's goal or purpose in life when he reaches middle age?"
"How can I understand my teen-ager better?"
"How does one work with a boss who doesn't listen?"

The one whose subject is chosen is asked to enlarge on his concern or topic. The group then spends sixty to ninety minutes discussing and listening to each other, using the topic as the basic ingredient for the laboratory experience.

Subjects Discussed Secondary

Often, the subjects chosen for discussion become the primary concern, with the group forgetting that the discussion subject is secondary to *how* they discuss the subject, as they listen to persons and not just to words. This usually occurs when the group becomes careless about reserving forty-five minutes at the close of the meeting for evaluation. Insight and growth in the art of listening as well as much of their self-discovery occurs mainly when the group "look at how" they discussed. The subject must always be of vital concern, but it is of necessity secondary.

On the other hand, some groups have difficulty because the subject chosen is of such general interest that the members do not feel strongly about it. When this happens, there are few feelings to listen to, and very little listening in depth occurs. While the subject chosen is secondary to the way it is discussed, it must be a subject eliciting real concern, and sometimes conflict, or there will be very little in the laboratory to observe.

The groups do not choose a predetermined theme. Subjects not discussed one evening are brought up the next if the person concerned still feels that it is a subject of real interest to him at that time. Whenever groups have planned to discuss a subject for the next meeting, it has lost its "nowness" and vitality by the time they meet again. Planned subject matter tends to make the group "teaching"-centered rather than "discovery"-centered where each person may look forward to a "happening" every evening arising from the current concerns and feelings of the members.

Leadership Shared

It is important to remember that each person is responsible for leadership in the group. Each tries to keep the group aware of the principles of listening summarized in the evaluation scale. Those less involved in a heated discussion should feel responsible to help the others to listen beyond words to feelings. Those naturally more sensitive help others to deeper insight throughout the evening and especially during the evaluation period.

New groups are formed by asking a couple with a year's experience in a group to "seed" another group. The pastor meets with the new group for six sessions and then drops in on the group from time to time at subsequent meetings to help them with problems they may be having.

People who seed the new groups get their training mainly from actual experience in a group for a year plus being with the pastor the first six meetings of the new groups. Seed couples meet with the pastor every three months to clear signals and raise concerns about their group's development. More research needs to be done on how best to equip the seed couples. One danger is in letting the seed people feel that they are the "leaders" of the group, and thus take away the responsibility of each member of the group to share the leadership. The best training of leadership is in the group as a whole when the pastor is with them the first six meetings, and then, when he visits the group occasionally, to go over the blocks and difficulties encountered.

The Role of the Pastor

Obviously, the pastor has the main responsibility for recruiting the group, the training of the seed couples, and the group as a whole in the principles of listening. He should be a person who has moved beyond the need to be an authority figure. Some pastors have great difficulty in this area, for they are trained to be "in charge" and feel most uncomfortable spending an evening where anything spontaneous might happen.

It is recommended that the pastor be in a group of his own which he and his wife attend regularly for their own growth and self-discovery. He needs this accepting, loving, mask-removing experience as much as his parishioners, and he is better equipped to help others to freedom and openness if he has the experience himself.

If a pastor invests three evenings a week, he can be active in six groups which meet twice a month. Our practice has been to start about three or four groups a year, remaining with the group for the first six evenings when the pastor's leadership is needed most.

Blocks Encountered

When Groups Become Too Supportive

Group members grow to like each other so well that they often become overly supportive of each other when someone wants honestly to face himself as he really is. Group members minimize his feelings to evade the pain he feels and the hurt it gives themselves to face it with him.

When Groups Become Ingrown

Groups can easily become ingrown as the members have shared and grown together over a long period of time. Their mutual acceptance and development in self-understanding can easily cause them to feel set apart from others in the church, and for others to set them apart.

This concern needs to be brought before the group periodically. When members are asked to "seed" new groups, their own growth may be shared with others.

Members need to be challenged with the church's mission outreach program regularly so that they can see their group's purpose as "preparing them for mission."

When Personal Counseling Is Needed

From time to time, a group member senses a need for personal counseling as a result of insight or the opening of new areas in his life. He may speak to his pastor, or his pastor may become aware of these changes and make it easy for him to pursue the discussion personally when they see each other on another occasion.

Potential serious difficulties in marriage often become evident in Listening Group discussion. The pastor needs to be aware of this so he may be helpful in providing another occasion for the counseling needed. Many such opportunities to help do not come to light through the average parish groups or organizations. "Seed" members should be trained and alerted to watch for these opportunities so they may be reported to the pastor if he is not in the group.

When Groups Hit Plateaus

Groups often hit plateaus in their movement toward depth in listening. After meeting for several months with members coming to enjoy each others' company more, it is easy to fall into the pattern of social groups. When this happens, more time should be given to the evaluation period of viewing the "laboratory" to see "how" they were listening and relating to each other.

The Loquacious Member

In almost every group, there is one individual who talks more than the others and will dominate the group unless the members help each other to be aware of their participation. Scale Number 3 used regularly will help the loquacious members be aware of their weakness. One evidence of the group's honesty and acceptance is to help a dominant member face realistically his negative role.

Sometimes silent members need to be encouraged to share their ideas, especially when they feel that what they have to say is not very important. On the other hand, some people do not need to say very much in order to participate fully and feel a vital part of the group.

When A Group Needs New Members

When members of the group move from the community or decide to drop out, it is important to start the group again following the pattern of the first three sessions described above. It is best to add three or four people at a time so that the new ones do not feel so "alone" during the first few meetings. A group can be reduced to nine from its maximum of twelve before it gets too small for efficiency.[6]

Conclusion

Most of the church renewal programs are calling for a rediscovery of the New Testament ministry of the laity. The Listening Group may be one human relations laboratory where laymen practice the art of loving and being loved. Before the laymen can be the "Man for Others" in this world as God's servant ministry, he needs to *experience* the "new life" relationship first hand. "We love because Christ first loved us."

Douglas Steere [7] has said, "To listen another soul into a condition of disclosure and discovery may be almost the greatest service a human being ever performs for another."

13. Educational Groups in the Church

KENNETH STOKES

Most of the interpersonal groups of the types described in this book arise outside the framework of traditional church programs, and are related to the church mainly through newly improvised channels. How can these groups function within the more conventional program of the church? Dr. Stokes, of the United Church of Christ in Gainesville, Florida, describes here the way in which a group approach has been developed by a vital and extensive adult education program, not simply in the structure of the program but in the basic philosophy underlying it.

The philosophy of our church's program is expressed verbally by what we like to describe as the triangle of church life—WORSHIP, EDUCATION, and OUTREACH. As the triangle is the fundamental geometric figure in architectural design, since its three sides are dependent one upon the other, so our church's program is based upon these three dimensions, all of which are mutually interdependent one upon the other.

Although this chapter focuses upon but one aspect of one of these three elements of the church's life—*adult education*—it is important that this be seen for its integral part in the larger context of the total program.

The United Church of Gainesville (United Church of Christ) was conceived in 1964 and formally organized in the spring of 1965 by a small group of people in this southern university city (the University of Florida is located in Gainesville) of approximately 60,000 permanent residents. From the first tentative meetings of the small group of concerned individuals, the need was felt and the desire expressed that there be a strong program of adult study and personal growth opportunity in addition to the usual activities of church life. The writer was called to be the first pastor of the church with this desire indelibly etched into his mind by the pulpit committee.

Many of the original (and subsequent) members of the church are a part of the University of Florida faculty, although an equal number come from a wide spectrum of the community's vocational roles. Most of the members are people who have a motivating intellectual interest in their religion. They are not content merely to sit and be told what to believe—they want to raise questions, to discuss, to hear someone else's ideas.

Beyond this intellectual concern is the desire to do more than just talk—to act! Consciously or unconsciously, this church seeks to be a *thinking* and a *doing* church, and out of this fundamental concern of the people from the beginning has come the program of adult seminars which involves nearly all of the more than one hundred adults who participate regularly in the life of the church.

The participants in the church's life from its beginning have been, for the most part, therefore, those who are genuinely searching for a vital faith and relevant meaning in their religion. Although many begin this search at the intellectual level, most find before long the necessity of a growing spiritual dimension in their lives. Some find this in the group experience, others find it in service activity, while still others are discovering new significance in prayer and the devotional life. Most will agree, however, that the beginning of this meaning has come in the experience of the adult seminars.

Structure

The present structure of our program was developed early in the life of the church when it was felt by many that there must be elements of the *worship* experience and the *educational* experience for both *children* and *adults* as a part of each Sunday morning's activity. The intensive focus on Sunday mornings arose from the recognition that it is difficult, if not impossible, to find a time when busy people in a typically over-organized community can have church activities together other than on Sunday morning. Whatever may be said about the increasing de-emphasis of Sunday as a day for the church, Sunday morning still remains the only time when the largest proportion of the church's membership can gather together for worship and study. Therefore, a new concept of Sunday morning activity was accepted by the congregation and all members agreed to participate during a trial period of six months.

This basic concept of our Sunday morning program is that *it is a two-hour unity of experiences for all ages*. Although no one is required to participate for the entire two-hour period, nearly 90 per cent of our people do so.

Our program also deviates from the traditional pattern in that the service of worship precedes, rather than follows the educational program. Instead of "bringing the children to Sunday School," then coming back an hour later for the church service, most of our adults come as families to worship and stay throughout the morning's activities.

We begin with *worship* for the entire family at 9:45 A.M. Children of school age come to the worship service with their parents. A brief Junior Sermon focuses on a particular interest for the children and emphasizes their participation in worship. Following the Junior Sermon and Offering, children through junior high age are free to leave, if they so desire, for an activity program. Some of the older children prefer to stay through the service of worship and they are encouraged to do so if and when they wish.

During the activity period for the children, the service of worship continues for adults and young people, most of this time being given to the reading of scripture, the sermon, and corporate prayer.

At approximately 10:35 A.M., fifty minutes after the service began, there is a "coffee break" for adults and "juice break" for the children. This is a time for discussing the ideas in the sermon, informal conversation, and just getting acquainted with new friends in the congregation. During this time, also, the facilities of our building are rearranged for the activities of the second hour.

The second hour, as it is called, begins at 10:55 and continues until 11:45 A.M. During this time, the church school classes for children meet, using regular church school curriculum material throughout, while the adult seminar program takes place at the same time.

Since our young people are confirmed and become full members of the church in the ninth grade, we consider those in high school to be a part of the adult seminar program, rather than of the church school. Although these teen-agers have a seminar of their own—directed to their particular interests— they often participate with the older adults in some of the seminars that are of particular interest to them. University students participate in the regular seminars with the rest of the adults.

Underlying Concept

Our program of adult seminars is based upon several premises stemming from our contemporary culture's increasing understanding of *adult learning* (please note that each of these premises builds successively upon those prior to it):

1. Adult education has become an accepted part of our society. Adults no longer shy away from the educational experience as something "just for children."
2. Increasingly, thinking adults want to learn more about their faith. They have mature questions that were not answered for them in their previous Sunday School experience and they want to find answers. They are deeply concerned at what they consider to be the irrelevance of the church in today's society. They are searching for ways to find a relevance they believe to be there.
3. The minister has ceased to be the authority figure he was even up to a generation ago. A college education has become a norm

and graduate education not uncommon among a large proportion of our church population. They are not content just to *listen* to a sermon. They are not content to hear someone *teach* a class. They want to participate in the growing experience. They too have something to contribute.

4. Adults today want to grapple with ideas in matters of faith and make their own decisions about their own beliefs.

5. Honest acceptance of our differences of religious interpretation is seen not as heresy or lack of faith, but rather as a positive and necessary prerequisite to the understanding of the larger spectrum of faith and belief and, more importantly, the individual's place within this spectrum.

It is upon these premises that the program of adult seminars was developed, and they underlie the planning and presentation of all seminars.

Variety of Seminars

An effort is made to provide a variety of learning experiences in two different ways. *First,* at least two or three seminars are offered concurrently, so that each adult can choose the one closest to his personal interest and need. *Second,* seminars continue for a specific period of time, usually six to eight weeks, after which a new group of seminars is offered. In this way, each person can participate in four or five different seminars during the period from September to June when seminars are offered.

Seminars are chosen on the basis of interest expressed by participants through periodic questionnaires and informal conversation, and leadership is developed in different ways. Some seminars are led by persons who are clearly knowledgeable in their fields—the pastor is called upon for Bible study and theological seminars, for example, while others in the congregation with particular areas of competence take leadership at these points of competence. Some of the seminars involve a series of outside speakers, each of whom makes a brief presentation which is followed by questions and discussion. Others are guided by laymen who serve primarily as moderators for the group's discussion of paperback books or other topics of common interest and concern.

Since individuals respond to different content and various types of group experience, extreme care is taken to make all seminars offered simultaneously as varied in terms of both these dimensions as possible. For example, during a given six- to eight-week period there probably will be a seminar dealing with Bible study, historical theology, church history, or some other area of our Judeo-Christian heritage. During the same period, a second seminar might focus primarily upon a contemporary problem or problems which are relevant to our Christian concern for society today. The third seminar, then, might be one of a personal enrichment nature, such as a discussion of matters of ethics or personal Christian living.

Concurrent seminars are, therefore, designed to have as wide a range of *content* as possible. At the same time, the attempt is also made to see that there is a variety in the *methodologies* employed. We have found that while some adults prefer a healthy discussion with a lot of "give-and-take," others like a larger emphasis on a directed presentation of material. The effort is always made, therefore, to provide both of these approaches, as well as combinations of the two during every seminar period.

During the two years that our adult seminars have been operating, a number of topics within the larger framework of religious study have been used and, to date, none has been repeated. We have never had the problem of finding topics for seminars. Our problem has been, rather, the finding of time to meet the varied interests involved and topics requested.

Seminar Topics

The essence of the United Church of Gainesville's adult seminar program can probably best be seen in a brief overview of the seminars held during the first two years of the program's existence. During most seminar periods, three seminars have met concurrently, although during some only two were held.

The first series of seminars, held in the early months of the church's existence, included:

"QUESTIONS CHILDREN ASK." Led by a thoughtful young couple of the church, this seminar, which was of particular interest to those with children, involved the discussion of ways to understand and answer children's questions about God, Jesus, Holy Spirit, Heaven and Hell, and the like.

"THE STORY OF THE CHRISTIAN CHURCH." This group was taught by the pastor and was essentially a survey of the development of Christianity from the time of Jesus to the present.

"THE CHRISTIAN IN THE CONTEMPORARY WORLD." Harvey Cox's Secular City was read and discussed under the moderatorship of two of the members of the congregation.

The response to the first seminar series was favorable, so several others were held during the winter and spring which included such topics as the following:

"OUR FELLOW RELIGIONS—JUDAISM AND CATHOLICISM." This seminar spent three weeks with each of these two major religious groups, drawing upon local speakers from each and stressing contemporary aspects in the light of the ecumenical movement.

"HONEST TO GOD." This group had little formal structure. Bishop Robinson's provocative little book was read and discussed under the guidance of a layman whose major responsibility was to moderate rather than teach.

"INTRODUCTION TO THE BIBLE." The pastor led this seminar, which was essentially a quick overview of the major sections and themes of the Bible.

"CONTEMPORARY CONCERNS FOR CHRISTIANS." The members of this seminar chose, at their first session, several topics of contemporary social concern—such as "Viet Nam," "Our Penal System," "Religion in the Public Schools," and "Contemporary Funeral Practices"— to be discussed in the light of our faith.

"OTHER PROTESTANT DENOMINATIONS." This seminar provided the opportunity for participants to become acquainted with the basic beliefs and procedures of several of the neighboring churches of our community.

"THE COMMON VENTURES OF LIFE." Paperback copies of the little book by D. Elton Trueblood of this title were purchased and read, and the major themes of the book—birth, marriage, vocation, and death—provided the bases for the Sunday morning discussions.

At the end of the first year of the adult seminar program, an evaluation was made, first in the form of a questionnaire filled out by all who had participated, and secondly by the Board of Education of the church, and submitted to the Church Council. The results of the evaluation indicated a whole-hearted response to the adult seminars and the clear-cut desire on the part of the people to continue with the program. On this basis, then, an overview of seminars for the entire second year was planned. This overview was followed, for the most part, and has given an overall balance to the program which has been most helpful. Some of the seminars held during the second year included:

"TILLICH." Under the leadership of a church member who had read widely among Tillich's writings, this group studied some of the theologian's shorter writings.

"INSIDE GAINESVILLE." This seminar directed itself to some of the educational, political, and social problems of our own community and was developed under the leadership of the church's Board of Outreach.

It should be noted that the question underlying this seminar was "What can our church do?" and the discussions and ideas which were generated have become important parts of the Board of Outreach's program.

"LIFE AND TEACHING OF JESUS." Under the guidance of the pastor, this group focused on the major elements of Jesus' ministry and the meaning of this ministry today.

"A CHRISTIAN RESPONSE TO MODERN FICTION." This group read some short works of fiction by Tolstoy, Ibsen, Dostoevski, Salinger, and others. A university professor, not a member of the church, led this seminar.

"WORLD RELIGIONS." A study in Islam, Buddhism, Hinduism, and Confucianism provided the basis of this seminar, which was led by one of our members who had been born and raised in the Orient.

"OLD TESTAMENT PROPHETS." The members of this seminar read from the prophets of Israel and, under the leadership of the pastor, explored their implications not only for their day but for ours.

"THE NEW MORALITY." Joseph Fletcher's book, *Situation Ethics*, provided the basis for another book discussion seminar moderated by one of the church members.

"HUMAN VALUES AND THE NEWLY DEVELOPING NATIONS." This seminar was developed with the major focus here on our church's concern with *world* problems.

"RETHINKING CHRISTIAN DOCTRINES." Led by a member of the church who quite honestly professed questions and doubts in matters of faith, this seminar explored some of the "stumbling blocks" to Christian belief: virgin birth, miracle, resurrection, and the like. Leslie Weatherhead's book, *The Christian Agnostic*, served as a resource for the group.

"CHRISTIANITY AND COMMUNISM." Drawing upon a number of resources in the field, this group sought to understand this most important political power struggle of our time.

Process

As can be seen from this review of some of our adult seminar topics, there has been a wide variety of seminars offered. This was done purposely to open up for the participants—many of whom had considered adult education in the church as something restricted primarily to Bible study—the rich varieties of areas of concern for Christians.

It can also be seen that various patterns of leadership have been involved. To assume that an adult group must have a "teacher" who will "instruct" is wrong. Adults do not always need to be "taught." Each participant brings something to the group that adds to the educational process.

We have found that simply reading a book together and discussing it can be a valuable learning experience. Similarly, the availability of persons able and willing to make presentations of significance and value within the framework of a seminar's overall theme is endless. For the most part, churches do not avail themselves enough of this kind of excellent leadership both inside and outside their congregational membership.

Our program has tried to present enough seminars at each period to keep the membership in each at less than twenty persons. For the most part this has been achieved. Persons are invited merely to attend the seminar of their choice and, by planning a balance of topics, the numerical distribution among seminars has been fairly even. We have also been pleased with the consistency of attendance, particularly when one remembers that most of our people have been inactive or outside church life in their recent years.

For the most part, however, the seminars which have featured a succession of speakers week after week and a "presentation-plus-question-and-answer" format have tended to be 1) larger in size, 2) more formal in procedure, and 3) more intellectually oriented than have those seminars which are more of a discussion nature and are led by the same person over a period of weeks.

Our observation has been that most of the persons relating to our program have been, initially, looking for an approach to religion that could be intellectually acceptable. Once they have found security at this point, they have begun to look more deeply for opportunities for richer interpersonal experience. For this reason, the church has tried to meet needs at those levels where such need is readily expressed, but *also* to stimulate the awareness of deeper needs which are not met by intellectual study and discussion alone, but can be approached only through an ongoing relationship of persons searching intimately together for meaning in life.

Since the seminars are changed every few weeks, this opportunity for seminar members to become deeply involved one with the other is not always possible. For this reason, although the Sunday morning seminars will no doubt continue, plans are being made for the development of ongoing groups, probably meeting in the evenings, in which the participants will have the opportunity for the deeper interpersonal relationship which cannot be totally fostered in the Sunday morning program.

The writer, as pastor of the church, has found that knowing

the individual interests and abilities of the members of the congregation has been most helpful in the finding of leadership for the seminars, some of which have been designed to fit the specialized abilities of members of the congregation. The seminar on Tillich, for example, grew basically out of the desire expressed on the evaluation questionnaire that this theologian be studied, but the fact that one of our members was known by the pastor to have read extensively and thoughtfully from among Tillich's works made the idea a realistic possibility. When approached, this man was glad to serve as leader of the group and was, therefore, given the freedom to develop the seminar in terms of his own abilities in its leadership.

Special Seminars

Although the six- to eight-week seminar series with two or three seminars being held simultaneously has provided the backbone of our adult seminar program, we have found several variations on the theme most helpful and worthwhile.

Between each six- to eight-week series, there are usually one or two Sundays on which special (we call them "one-shot") seminars are held for all adults. These have included "talk-back" sessions for the discussion of the pastor's sermon of the day, usually on topics of discussable interest. Two of the more popular of these "talk backs" took place after sermons on the "God is Dead" theology and on the report of the Consultation on Church Union.

Since some of the natural breaking points for seminar series come at the holiday times of Christmas and Easter, we have utilized some of these Sundays for seminars appropriate to the season. One Christmas, for example, a student from the United Church of South India told of Christmas customs in his country, while on another mid-December Sunday, a representative of the Jewish community was with us to discuss the major Jewish holidays.

Another variation has been the *Sermon and Seminar Series* in which, on a series of consecutive Sundays, both the sermon and the seminar for *all* adults have been addressed to the same topic as a part of a larger theme for the entire period. One three-week *Sermon and Seminar Series,* for example, concerned itself with the theme, "The Church's Concern with the Issues of Today," and included as specific topics for each of the three Sundays: *politics, racial ferment,* and *the scientific revolution.* On each of these Sundays, the sermon during the worship service was a theological orientation to the issue chosen for that day. During the second hour, a discussion of this issue was continued in more specific form—a presentation by our representative to the state legislature (politics), an excellent film on civil rights (racial ferment), and a panel of medical doctors discussing some of the moral and ethical problems in their field (scientific revolution). Good publicity of these topics in the local press resulted in a large number of visitors both at our services of worship and in our seminar sessions on those Sundays.

Results

Since the adult seminar program began, our participation in the seminars has been numerically between 80 and 90 per cent of the adults attending the service of worship. Although we try to emphasize our philosophy of a total program of *both* worship and educational experience for all ages, we do not and, of course, cannot *require* participation in both aspects of the program. Actually, while there are some people who attend worship and do not stay for seminars, we have found this number to be just about offset by those who come to the second hour just for the seminars. This does not trouble us, for some of these latter are those for whom the formality of worship has lost its meaning. If these people find in the seminar the beginning of a renewed religious faith, we are happy to have them participate to whatever extent they so desire at this time in their lives. Many who started by coming just to the seminars have begun to find in the dimension of worship the *next* step in their growing faith.

We have been happily surprised at the number of people from other churches who have participated in our seminars. Several have indicated that they have no thought of leaving their own churches, but wish to take part in a specific series which is of interest to them. Our publicity in the local press stresses the fact that any who so desire are welcome to participate in the seminars.

Limiting each seminar to six, seven, or eight weeks has its drawbacks, to be sure. There is obviously less group involvement in this setup than there is in a group which meets together for a longer period of time. The fact that many topics cannot easily be covered in such a short time is also a problem, although it is usually not too difficult to subdivide a larger area of concern into two or more units, each of which can be covered in a specific seminar period.

On the other hand, there are several important advantages to this time limitation. Persons asked to lead seminars, be they church members or outsiders, are more willing to accept the responsibility on a volunteer basis if the time period involved is not overly lengthy. The relatively short periods of time make possible a variety of experiences for each participant in the course of a year. It has been found that too long a time spent on a topic can tend to become wearying and often leads to increasing absenteeism. For that matter, many people are willing to make a commitment of regular attendance for a relatively short period of time which they probably would hesitate to make to a group which meets indefinitely.

Another problem has come in the recruiting of teachers for the church school. Since the church school and adult seminars meet at the same time, teaching in the former has meant that participation in the seminar program is not possible. For this reason, church school teachers are now recruited for periods of time which coincide with the time periods of the seminar series. In this way, church school leadership rotates throughout the year with each teacher serving approximately two months. Although some persons have feared that this would have a negative effect on the church school classes, this has not been the case. The children seem to respond to the vitality of periodic new leadership and we are rapidly developing a roster of well over half our membership who have had experience in the church school.

Evaluation

As this is written, our church has still had less than two years' experience with our adult seminar program. Already new ideas and suggestions are being raised which may well change and, hopefully, improve it in the years ahead. But this is good, for in this day and age of rapid change, all things must be adaptable to new needs and new opportunities.

However, we do feel that the basic concept of the adult seminars—which urges adults to think, to talk, to disagree, and to grow together in matters of their religious faith—is a valid one. We believe that the variety of offerings expands our participation, and we feel strongly that there is a definite value in changing the groupings every few weeks, so that group membership does not become static and crystallized with the same people saying essentially the same thing week after week. At the same time, however, we are becoming increasingly aware of the important function of ongoing groups, so are more and more seeking to develop these in our church in addition to the seminars.

14. Living Room Dialogues

WILLIAM B. CATE

The spirit of ecumenism liberated by the Vatican Council finds a "grass-roots" expression in the rise of the "Living Room Dialogue" groups described here. Beginning as a venture in the exploration of mutal beliefs and attitudes, these groups often move on to become primary communities in themselves, and to engage in mission outreach. Dr. Cate is Executive Secretary of the Greater Portland (Oregon) Council of Churches, and author, among other titles, of *The Ecumenical Scandal on Main Street*.

Living Room Dialogues * are, in the words of a Roman Catholic laywoman, the means through which "we have rediscovered and acknowledged that other Christians are Christians, sharing a common baptism and faith. It is this discovery that has led us into a deeper study of our doctrines and of scripture with a resulting increase in our observance and devotion to our tradition. We find ourselves becoming familiar with so much that we had carelessly concluded was too deep for us. We find ourselves enlightened and enlightening as we speak and listen and learn together."

What Are the Living Room Dialogues?

The dialogues are an effort to give systematic direction to a spontaneous grass-roots desire among many lay people to be-

* The writer was assisted in writing this paper by three lay participant observers who were members of three different Living Room Dialogue groups. Much that is recorded here comes from the careful records of their experience in the groups. They are Mrs. Arnold L. Leech, Episcopal; Mrs. Robert K. Anderson and John Baranov, Roman Catholic.

come involved in the ecumenical movement at the point of discussion or conversation about religious issues related to Christian unity. The effort was initiated by the Rev. William B. Greenspun, C.S.P., who is the National Director, Apostolate of Goodwill of the Confraternity of Christian Doctrine of the Roman Catholic Church. He secured the cooperation of the Rev. William A. Norgren, Executive Director, Department of Faith and Order of the National Council of Churches of Christ in developing resource literature which took the form of a paperback entitled "Living Room Dialogues." [1] This guide has been made available to local communities throughout the nation. At this writing over 150,000 copies of the paperback guides have been sold and another discussion guide on Christian community responsibility has been prepared.

The stated purpose of the dialogue program is to help individual laymen and women become personally concerned about Christian unity and to pray for the reunion of all Christians. In addition, the program aims to remove confusion and misunderstanding among the laity of different Christian traditions and to nourish understanding and appreciation for the faith and worship of each other's church.

The program came to Portland, Oregon, early in 1966 after a pilot program in Worcester, Massachusetts. The ground had been well prepared for its reception in our city by theological discussion about unity that had taken place among a limited number of Roman Catholic and Protestant clergy and laity during a prior four-year period. The earliest regional faith and order conference in the United States had taken place in the Pacific Northwest in 1961. Most of the laity had heard of this conference or had taken part in an annual Public Gathering for Prayers for Christian Unity held for three years during the Week of Prayer for Christian Unity in January.

It was decided at a meeting of representative Protestant and Catholic clergy and laity called together by the Greater Portland Council of Churches that some coordination would be needed in order that everyone who was interested in the Living Room Dialogues would have an opportunity to participate.

Seven persons at this gathering were named the Living Room Dialogue Coordinating Committee. The city was divided into fifteen large neighborhoods. A Protestant and Catholic clergy coordinator in the area was arbitrarily chosen. In most areas the clergy then formed a lay committee and participants were recruited from a wide variety of churches in order to make the dialogues dynamic with a rich diversity of traditions. There was no noticeable difference in enthusiasm for the program predicated on socioeconomic differences. Some inner city areas did as well as some suburban areas. In our city, over three thousand lay people enrolled in the dialogues. The continuing role of the Living Room Dialogue Coordinating Committee was to serve as a general supervisor of the program and kept up communication to areas through periodic mailings.

At an orientation session the lay people in each area were divided into small groups of twelve to fifteen people, making sure each group had representatives from as many traditions as possible. The groups meet in the homes of members for the seven dialogues which the paperback resource book contains. In our city we added one additional facet to the program that proved helpful. In cooperation with the state-operated educational television station, we scheduled seven television programs on the second Monday of the month at 7:30–8:00 P.M. This program provided a discussion starter for groups that could meet on that night. The station used its own director to develop the programs. The coordinating committee of the dialogue served as the planning committee for the programs, which were related to the dialogue for the month as contained in the study guide. The television programs have resulted in a widespread vicarious involvement in the dialogues by people who were not able to be a part of a dialogue group. Many viewers have already indicated that they want to be involved in future opportunities.

The Structure of the Dialogues

The genius of the Living Room Dialogues seems, first of all, to be their small-group, informal nature. Informality is reinforced by the fact that they are held in homes, not in churches. The seven-month period over which the dialogues are held allows for the establishment of intimate relationships among the members of a small group.

The second important characteristic of the dialogues is that they are composed entirely of lay people. The exclusion of the clergy makes possible a freedom of thought and expression that otherwise would not occur. The Living Room Dialogues have dispelled, in this writer's mind, the former illusion that lay people need a trained theological leader to discuss theological issues.

In the dialogues the clergyman serves as a resource person in between sessions. The way this occurred varied in the different areas. In one locality the lay coordinators met monthly with the clergy in the churches involved to discuss problems arising out of the dialogues. In other areas the clergymen were consulted on an individual basis by leaders or members of groups. The regular meeting of clergy and lay coordinators of the dialogues in an area seemed from our experience to be the best way for the clergy to be involved. The dialogue appeared to prosper more in the areas where this kind of systematic coordination occurred.

The third most distinguishing characteristic of the dialogues are their interchurch nature. The dialogues provide a place of meeting for individual Christians from Christian traditions that have been isolated from each other for centuries. Many lay participants are drawn to the dialogues because of their curiosity about what other communions actually believe and are like if known intimately. The three lay people who have helped supply data for this paper all witness to what this new communication means in terms of a surprising Christian joy and new-found freedom in the one Lord of the Church and away from spiritually crippling misconceptions, stereotypes, and inherited fears from the past. Through the dialogues Christian people are able to free each other. They find that they cannot free themselves from the circumscribed constraining bonds of their separated Christian tradition.

In church circles locally there is a growing aversion to any nationally promoted church programming. However, the non-promotional manner in which the Living Room Dialogue program was made available to communities dispelled this potential danger in the program. The paperback resource book is the chief organizing agent around which the dialogues have been developed. Reports from groups indicate that the book is used in a variety of ways by different groups. Some, unfortunately, follow it in almost a rote manner. Others simply ask participants to read material in advance and then formulate their own monthly program. Most groups, however, use the paperback freely as a resource from which they read but not as an infallible guide. The subjects of the dialogues in the first Living Room Dialogue paperback indicate the type of issues dealt with in the dialogues:

Dialogue No. 1   Concern, Prayer, Love: Foundation for Dialogue
Dialogue No. 2   Good Conversation in Christ
Dialogue No. 3   How Do We Worship?
Dialogue No. 4   Our Common Christian Heritage
Dialogue No. 5   Renewal of God's People
Dialogue No. 6   Our Common Christian Witness
Dialogue No. 7   Why We Don't Break Bread Together

The usual procedure in the dialogue is to begin with the suggested prayers and Bible readings. This is followed by a section entitled "Christian Dialogue," which provides discussion material for the meeting. Often, in our city, the television program has provided the initial spark to set the conversation going and brings in insights and information relevant to our own particular situation. After the dialogue is under way, the main task is to keep group process moving in a good dialogical fashion. The most difficult thing for people to do is to learn to listen to others.

Although Father Greenspun in his directions for the organization of the group suggested that in choosing a leader groups should consider co-leaders—a Roman Catholic and a Protestant, a man and a woman—what has actually happened in most groups is that dialogues have chosen a permanent chairman and usually a man. Generally speaking, the group leaders were given no special directions in conducting the groups other than the general guideline for discussion contained in the introduction of the study guide. Looking back on the program, this is probably one of the places where it should be strengthened in the future. The chief saving factor here for the program was that it seemed to attract the more alert and experienced lay people in the various churches. Therefore, leadership potential in the groups was high.

The Functioning of the Dialogue

Let us reconstruct the setting for a typical Living Room Dialogue group meeting as it has been conveyed to the writer by lay participants. On the opening night eleven out of fifteen members of the group attended the meeting. It was held in the home of an Episcopal couple. Present were five Roman Catholics, two Presbyterians, two Episcopalians, one Lutheran, and one Methodist. At the first meeting an air of expectancy pervaded the atmosphere, but also noticeable was a caution and reserve that characterizes people meeting for the first time. The group began with each person identifying his church relationship, his work, and special interests. After this general introduction they proceeded directly into the dialogue. Following is the report of the first meeting of one group as reported by a participant:

> Virgil (a Catholic layman selected as chairman of the group) began by asking that an answer be given to questions in the study guide. He proceeded by calling on individuals in order of their seating arrangement. Although there was some response, I spoke about the arrangement feeling that spontaneous thoughts are more fruitful to a dialogue group. Others agreed and the rest of the evening was done in a less formal fashion and with better response. The

leader was careful to limit the dialogue to 9:30 P.M. and, therefore, moved along rapidly through the outline.

The author has noted one rather widespread concern expressed by some Protestant laymen prior to the first session and in some cases even after it, which was that the Catholics might seek to dominate the dialogues. After the second session, however, this apprehension was never expressed again. In fact, the second meetings, as well as the subsequent meetings, were marked by a happiness at seeing each other again and also a growing excitement that in the dialogue they had "a tiger by the tail." One participant characterized it this way: "They felt caught up in a movement not of their own personal motivation." Or as another participant stated it, "the Church doesn't belong to the clergy. As laity, they have power and, in fact, are the Church."

An analysis of the experience of the participants indicates certain types of interaction occurring as they confront each other.

1. *An Effort to Establish Common Ground*

As is generally believed, the initial tendency of the dialogue group is not to define differences. In the beginning the group seeks to establish common ground in order to justify its existence. This common ground is usually stated in terms of the allegiance to a common Lord, Jesus Christ. It may also center around the group's common task as Christians in the world or the fact that our scandalous divisions hurt all Christianity. A Catholic participant said, "It was settled early that we must present a common Christian witness to be able to have any influence in the community." Another participant said, "Non-Christians look at us to get an idea of what Christianity is like. They are not particularly impressed. It seems to me that our divisions have kept us from becoming whole Christians." Still another participant said, "We're too busy polishing our own images to care much about the rest of the world." The first act of the group is to establish a common basis for relationship.

2. *Freedom to Question*

Catholics express long-held questions concerning the fact that Protestants move easily from Protestant church to Protestant church. They interpret this as indifference. Similarly, a Presbyterian layman wanted "to sit down with some Roman Catholics to see what makes them as they are, especially, what makes them go to church every Sunday." One observer reported that "most Protestants think the Roman Catholic cannibalistic in regard to transubstantiation. Ivan and Theresa, a Catholic couple, looked taken back and wordless." An Anglican member of a group was surprised to find that other members of the dialogue thought that King Henry the Eighth had started the Anglican Church. In the dialogue long-held questions, often impregnated with prejudice, are aired in the group.

3. *Elimination of False Stereotypes*

A next stage in the dialogical process is the developing realization that stereotypes held by members of the group are unreal and inherited from an insulated Protestant or Catholic religious ethos. An Episcopal laywoman admitted her past prejudice against certain Protestant denominations that celebrate Holy Communion so rarely. "But now," she said, "I realize that Jesus did not say do this every week in remembrance of me." A Presbyterian layman commented that the Second Vatican Council and involvement in his dialogue group had "changed a lot of his thinking regarding Catholicism." He reported that he was beginning to see the variety of belief and attitudes held by those within the Roman Catholic Church. Through the dialogue groups Catholics are beginning to realize that Protestants are developing increasing interest in liturgy and Protestants are beginning to understand that Catholics have a renewed interest in the scriptures. A Catholic dialogue participant said, "We feel we can express what we sense about religious beliefs without creating misunderstandings. . . . There is concurrence in our group that what we have in common is more important than our divisions."

4. *Strengthening of Personal Christian Identification*

A Catholic lady testified that it was through the interpersonal process in the intimate context of the Living Room Dialogues that she had had an experience of coming alive as a Christian. Her faith has become more personal and experiential as she has tried to articulate it to others and has been compelled by her involvement in the dialogue to reflect upon it. Other members of the dialogue have described the personal aspect of the dialogue experience in terms almost equivalent to a religious conversion. The more theologically sophisticated of the laity speak of the presence of Christ when two or three are met in His Name. From the author's perspective the most important aspect of the Living Room Dialogues is not the resolution of theological differences or the breaking down of religious institutional barriers, but the fact that it provides the occasion for the renewal of commitment by Christian lay people. They are motivated by their involvement to a process of maturation in the Christian faith and life.

5. *The Desire to Know More About One's Own Tradition*

One of the common arguments against interchurch dialogue among lay people is that it will dilute their faith and contribute to indifferentism. Analysis of the actual situation indicates that this is an unfounded fear. What actually happens in the dialogue is that they become aware of their own lack of knowledge of their tradition. In the periods between the monthly dialogue they do extensive reading about their own tradition. After her first dialogue meeting, a Methodist laywoman asked her pastor for a crash reading program on Methodism. She said that in her group she felt like a religious illiterate as regards to her own tradition.

The experience of this lady is the normal one in the Living Room Dialogues. Not only are the laity motivated to investigate their own tradition, but in the dialogue they are also compelled to clarify their own beliefs which are, all too often, held obscurely or lightly. The dialogues do not seek to indoctrinate the lay participants in some amorphous ecumenical theology. The statement of a Catholic laywoman expresses very clearly what happens:

> Having gone beyond what was the surprising area of like belief, which by the way made the foundation of my own faith so much broader, I am now able to face and accept with respect the areas of difference. Seeing the differences for what they are I realize that our distinctiveness is real. Many of the differences seem to be deep convictions held not only in our intellects but in our emotions. I don't believe they can be easily overcome but I also don't think many of them will have to be. They somehow have little relationship to essential faith.

6. The Desire to Continue the Groups

Members of the Living Room Dialogue groups cherish the warmth of this meaningful fellowship. It is a type of fellowship that they have rarely, if ever, experienced in their own parish or congregation. The following excerpt from the diary of one of the persons who kept a record of the happenings in their dialogue is illustrative: "At 9:30 Ivan, the chairman, politely said, 'I suppose we should be going.' They talked for another forty minutes and still were not ready to leave. As they went out the door, Wayne turned to us and said, 'I want you all to know how glad I am that I came!'" The lay coordinator of the dialogues in our city reports an overwhelming number of requests from groups for additional resource material, in order that they can continue their groups in the fall. Christian *koinonia* becomes real to them in the small group and they dislike leaving it and returning to the formal institutional style that characterizes much of the life of the local congregation.

The quality of friendship developed in the group, in most cases, grew far beyond the concern about ecclesiastical matters. Conversation before and after the formal context of the meetings often dealt with family problems and other very personal concerns. Many warm and continuing friends have arisen out of the groups. They have led to invitations to attend functions in each others churches, to go out to dinner, or attend some community function together. The dialogue groups have become for many people a place of warm human understanding and acceptance.

Results of the Living Room Dialogues

I have already alluded to the personal Christian renewal that takes place in the lives of lay people who participate in the dialogues. The critical question about the dialogues concerns whether they motivate the laity to become involved in the mission of the Church in the world.[2] Is the beginning and the end of the dialogues only empty talk?

Our experience in Portland has been that the dialogues usually lead to action. In one area of our city the dialogue groups are developing a church-community action program through which they will provide the creative center to pull the various facets of the community together to work at the resolution of community needs. In other areas of our city where neighborhood church-community action programs have already begun, the director claims that the dialogues have motivated many lay people to get involved in the community outreach of the church.

It is too early to tell what concrete results the dialogues will have in helping to renew the internal life of the congregation. I have not observed or have had reported to me any growth in indifferentism or lack of church interest by the lay people who have participated in the dialogues. It would be my projection that many congregations will be challenged to new levels of commitment and renewal by the laity who have come to understand Christ and His Church more fully through the dialogues. In our city we have experienced a few cases of clerical fear of the dialogues that take place outside their immediate control. On the whole, however, the clergy have welcomed the dialogues and have seen them to be a spiritually enlivening experience for their lay people.

An experience typical of many renewed lay people who have

participated in the dialogues is reflected by this Episcopal lay-woman:

> I was thinking about what a fine churchman I had been these past 20 years. My family was regular in church attendance. I was always ready to make the coffee and cook beans, scrub the church steps, plan a good program, teach church school, call upon a new parishioner or be an enthusiastic delegate to a convention. But I was wondering if I could measure up to this new Christianity. Could I sit with the alcoholic, be kind to the peddler at my door, touch the beggar on the street, or even be a better mother? Could I really love as He had loved?

We cannot know what means God will choose to renew His church. From what I have observed, however, this new inter-church dialogue among lay people may well become the dynamic that will transform the church in our time.

Notes

Chapter 1: The Rise of Interpersonal Groups—John L. Casteel

1. Paul A. Hare, *Handbook of Small Group Research.* New York: The Free Press, 1962, p. v.
2. Charles Horton Cooley, *Social Organization.* New York: Schocken Books, 1963, p. 23.
3. The rationale for this shift from the single executive to the management group if given by John K. Galbraith, *The New Industrial State.* Boston: Houghton Mifflin Co., 1967. Chapter VI.
4. William J. J. Gordon, *Synectics.* New York: Harper and Row, 1961.
5. Ruth Moore, *Niels Bohr: The Man, His Science, and the World They Changed.* New York: Alfred A. Knopf, 1966.
6. Edward LeRoy Long, *A Survey of Christian Ethics.* New York: Oxford University Press, 1967, p. 314.
7. As examples of a rapidly expanding literature, see W. R. Bion, *Experiences in Groups.* London: Tavistock Publications, 1959; Joseph Knowles, *Group Counseling.* Englewood Cliffs, N.J.: Prentice-Hall, 1964; Hobart Mowrer, *The New Group Therapy.* New York: D. Van Nostrand Co., 1964.
8. Hare, *op. cit.,* p. vii. See his table showing the increase in the number of bibliographical items appearing since 1890.
9. Boston: D. C. Heath, 1910. See especially Chapter VI.
10. *The New State.* New York: Longmans, 1918. *Creative Experience.* New York: Longmans, 1924.
11. New York: Association Press, 1928.
12. New Haven: Yale University Press, 1936, pp. 25–26.
13. London: Faber and Faber, 1961.
14. Gordon W. Allport, "Foreword," in *Resolving Social Conflicts,* ed. Gertrude Weiss Lewin. New York: Harper and Row, 1948, p. ix.
15. Dean E. Woodridge, *The Machinery of Life.* New York: McGraw-Hill, 1966, p. 8.
16. Weston LaBarre, *The Human Animal.* Chicago: University of Chicago Press, 1956, pp. 287, 302.
17. Among other titles, see Jacques Ellul, *The Technological Society.* New York: Alfred A. Knopf, 1964; John K. Galbraith, *The New Industrial State; Daedalus: Journal of the American Academy of Arts and Sciences* (Summer 1967), Vol. 96, No. 3.

18. *The Interpersonal Theory of Psychiatry.* New York: W. W. Norton, 1953, p. 6.

19. *Motivation and Personality.* New York: Harper and Row, 1954, p. 27.

20. Published by the Creative Education Foundation, Buffalo, New York.

21. *The Quest for Community.* New York: Oxford University Press, 1953, p. 231.

22. For a full discussion of "ontocratic" cultures and the problems they present to Christianity, see Arend Th. van Leeuwen, *Christianity in World History.* London: Edinburgh House, 1964, esp. pp. 13–45, and pp. 158–173.

23. *The Future of Belief.* New York: Herder & Herder, 1966. This section is largely indebted to Dewart's radical analysis of the current theological situation.

24. *Ibid.,* p. 145 n.

25. Chris Argyris, *Organization and Innovation.* Homewood, Ill.: Richard D. Irwin, 1965, p. 11. Findings in this study suggest important applications to educational and religious institutions as well as corporations.

26. *Understanding Media: The Extensions of Man.* New York: McGraw-Hill, 1965, pp. 5, 82, 255, 183.

27. See Chapter 4.

Chapter 3: Interpersonal Groups and the Church—Theodore O. Wedel

1. Cited in Colin W. Williams, *John Wesley's Theology Today.* Nashville, Tenn.: Abingdon Press, 1960, p. 151.

2. Yves M. J. Congar, *Lay People in the Church.* Westminster, Maryland: Newman Press, 1959, p. 51.

3. *Ibid.,* p. 45.

4. Essay by Robert Michaelsen in *The Ministry in Historical Perspective.* New York: Harper and Row, 1956, p. 284.

5. Emil Brunner, *The Misunderstanding of the Church.* Philadelphia: The Westminster Press, 1955.

6. Paul Tillich, *Systematic Theology.* Chicago: University of Chicago Press, 1951, Vol. I, p. 176.

7. Rudolf Bultman, "Grace and Freedom" in *Essays Philosophical and Theological.* London: S.C.M. Press, 1955, pp. 170–172.

8. Donald J. Ernsberger, *A Philosophy of Adult Christian Education.* Philadelphia: The Westminster Press, 1959, p. 145.

9. Adolf Harnack, *The Expansion of Christianity in the First Three Centuries,* trans. James Moffatt. New York: G. P. Putnam's Sons, 1905, Vol. II, p. 50.

Chapter 5: Elements of Group Behavior—Eugene E. Laubach

1. *Group Development,* at $2.00, in the Selected Reading Series published by the National Training Laboratories, National Education Associa-

tion, 1201 16th Street, N.W., Washington, D.C. Other valuable publications in this series include: *Leadership in Action, Human Forces in Teaching and Learning*, and *Forces in Community Development*.

Chapter 6: Personality Changes in Groups—Quentin Hand

1. J. P. Guilford and Wayne S. Zimmerman, *The Guilford-Zimmerman Temperament Survey*. Beverly Hills, Calif.: Sheridan Supply Company, 1949.
2. All names uesd are fictitious. Events and dates have been altered to protect identity.

Chapter 7: Preaching and Small Groups—Clyde Reid

1. See Theodore O. Wedel's article, "Is Preaching Outmoded?", in *Religion in Life* (Autumn 1965). Dr. Wedel cites some of the current debate on this issue.
2. John L. Casteel, ed., *Spiritual Renewal Through Personal Groups*. New York: Association Press, 1957, p. 44.
3. *Ibid.*, p. 119.
4. Letter to the author from John L. Casteel.
5. Wilbur Schramm, "Procedures and Effects of Mass Communication," in *Mass Media and Education*, ed. Nelson B. Henry. Chicago: University of Chicago Press, 1954, p. 113.
6. Melvin L. DeFleur and Otto N. Larsen, *The Flow of Information: An Experiment in Mass Communication*. New York: Harper and Row, 1958, pp. 22–23.
7. Reuel L. Howe, *The Miracle of Dialogue*. Greenwich, Conn.: The Seabury Press, 1963, p. 32.
8. This research is reported in detail in my Th.D. dissertation, "Two-way Communication through Small Groups in Relation to Preaching," Boston University, 1960.
9. For a more detailed report see my article, "Preaching and the Nature of Communication," *Pastoral Psychology* (October 1963).
10. For a scholarly discussion of these levels of communication, see George R. Bach, *Intensive Group Psychotherapy*. New York: The Ronald Press, 1954, pp. 275–293. Bach distinguishes seven levels of communication.

Chapter 8: The Counseling Group—Joseph W. Knowles

1. The counselor's qualifications and the dangers inherent in group counseling are to be discussed later. The group counselor needs to be an expert; the type of counseling described here should not be attempted by well-meaning persons who have no training for this task.
2. A fuller response to this question can be found elsewhere. See Joseph W. Knowles, *Group Counseling* in Successful Pastoral Counseling

Series, ed. Russell L. Dicks. Englewood Cliffs, N.J.: Prentice-Hall, 1964, pp. 25–38.

Bibliography

Helen I. Driver, *et al. Counseling and Learning Through Small Group Discussion.* Madison, Wis.: Monona-Driver Book Co., 1962.

Thomas Gordon, *Group Centered Leadership.* Boston: Houghton Mifflin Co., 1956.

Joseph W. Knowles, *Group Counseling.* Englewood Cliffs, N.J.: Prentice-Hall, 1964.

Rudolph Wittenberg, *So You Want to Help People.* New York: Association Press, 1947.

Chapter 9: Growth in Receptivity—Robert M. Cox

1. James V. Clark, "Toward a Theory and Practice of Religious Experiencing," in *Challenges of Humanistic Psychology*, Bugental. New York: McGraw-Hill, 1967.

Chapter 10: Professional Interpersonal Groups— Conrad Sommer

1. New York: International Universities Press, 1957.

Chapter 11: Parish Occupational Groups—Robert Batchelder and James Campbell

1. A most helpful discussion of the meaning of action is to be found in Hannah Arendt, *Human Condition.* Chicago: University of Chicago Press, 1958.
2. A concise guide outlining how pastor and laymen can organize parish occupational groups in a local congregation is available from the Detroit Industrial Mission, 8646 Puritan Avenue, Detroit, Michigan, 48238.

Chapter 12: Listening to Others—Robert A. Edgar

1. Robert A. Edgar, "The Listening Structured Group," *Pastoral Psychology* (June 1964).
2. Russell J. Becker, *Family Pastoral Care.* Englewood Cliffs, N.J.: Prentice-Hall, 1965, pp. 40–62.
3. This procedure is described on pp. 178 ff.
4. *On Listening to Another.* New York: Harper and Row, 1955, p. 6.

5. Copies of this Evaluation Scale are available from the author, % the publishers.
6. Becker, *op. cit.*, pp. 59–61.
7. Steere, *op. cit.*, p. 14.

Chapter 14: Living Room Dialogues—William B. Cate

1. The paperback study guide, *Living Room Dialogues* ($1.00), is obtainable at most standard religious bookstores or by ordering direct from the National Council of Churches, 475 Riverside Drive, New York, N.Y., 10027; or from the Paulist Press, Glen Rock, New Jersey. A second volume, *Second Living Room Dialogues,* is also available.
2. *Second Living Room Dialogues* focuses on Christians' involvement in current affairs in the secular world.